Life in the Pinball Machine

Observations from an Accidental Life in Learning and Human Performance

Careening from There to Here

For
Alisha Wirt

Bob Mager
10/1/03

Life in the Pinball Machine

Observations from an
Accidental Life in Learning
and Human Performance

Careening from
There to Here

Robert F. Mager

CEP Press
A wholly owned subsidiary of
The Center for Effective Performance, Inc.
Atlanta, Georgia

OTHER BOOKS PUBLISHED BY CEP PRESS

The New Mager Six-Pack, by Robert F. Mager

Preparing Instructional Objectives, Third Edition, by Robert F. Mager

Analyzing Performance Problems, Third Edition,
by Robert F. Mager & Peter Pipe

How to Make Smart Decisions About Training,
by Paul G. Whitmore, Ph.D.

CEP Press is a wholly owned subsidiary of The Center for Effective
Performance, Inc. (CEP), a consulting organization that specializes in
helping organizations improve performance.

For more information, contact:
CEP Press
2300 Peachford Rd.
Suite 2000
Atlanta, GA 30338
www.ceppress.com
(770) 458-4080 or (800) 558-4CEP

Library of Congress Cataloging-in-Publication Data
Mager, Robert Frank, 1923-
    Life in the pinball machine : careening from there to here / Robert F.
Mager.
        p. cm.
Includes bibliographical references and index.
    ISBN 0-9709527-2-4 (pbk. : alk. paper)
    1. Mager, Robert Frank, 1923- 2. Educators—Biography. 3. Learning,
Psychology of. 4. Performance. 5. Achievement motivation. I. Title.
    LB1060.M322 2003
    370'.92—dc21
                                        2002155916

Printed in the United States of America
09 08 07 06 05 04 03 10 9 8 7 6 5 4 3 2 1

Contents

Foreword

"Bob Mager changed my life."

I've heard that sentence so many times over the years, at professional conferences, from clients, fellow practitioners, teachers, and any number of other people who've happened onto his work and been amazed by its power and relevance.

I'm not the only person to have heard about his impact on people's lives. Several years ago, *Training Magazine* did a survey in which they asked training professionals an unusual question: If you were the first training director on the moon, and you could have the phone number of only one person to ask for help, whose would it be? The overwhelming choice? Bob Mager's.

So it is no exaggeration to say he has changed people's lives—learners' lives and performance improvement people's lives alike—and no surprise to hear so many people say it. Yet as I sat down to begin writing this foreword, it became clear that a list of accomplishments recognized or books sold would fall short of capturing what so desperately needed to be voiced – and that is to say what sets Mager apart. What is it about this man that has enabled him to have such an impact on so many people?

This book answers that question; it tells you how it all happened. It is a career chronicle, so to speak. It takes you behind the scenes and lets you see for yourself what makes him, and his way of thinking, unique. In the 30-plus years I've known Bob, I've never known him to take shortcuts. He simply takes care to do it right. He practices what he preaches—a rare thing in this surface-and-glitz oriented world. The process of learning—for Mager—is about more than instructing others. He is a perpetual learner, whether he's taking on unicycle-riding, juggling, tap dancing, or writing novels. That's part of why his work and his methodology resonate with learners to the degree that they do. He never forgets what it is to be a learner, because he continually puts himself in that position.

One of the biggest distinctions about his work is that it treats the learner with dignity. Bob is passionate about his desire to see students treated more humanely, a passion that's manifested in all of his work. That's why his books get read, and borrowed, and borrowed by someone else. I've never seen another instructional methodology that treats the learner that way. People act as if the objective of education should be to separate the wheat from the chaff; Mager says the objective of education should be for all learners to acquire the skills that are being taught. Isn't the purpose that *everyone* should get it?

Whether you're referring to his consulting work, books, speeches, or industry-standard workshops, here you have an individual who's had a mammoth impact on training and human performance. His ten books have been translated into seventeen languages and have sold over four million copies worldwide. *Preparing Instructional Objectives*, for example, published first in 1962 and in its third edition by 1997, continues to sell thousands of copies every year—forty years after its first printing—and was named one of the hundred most influential books of the twentieth century. He was a first-round inductee into Training Magazine's HRD Hall of Fame and a recipient of ISPI's Distinguished Professional Achievement Award, among others.

These ideas, approaches, products, and books didn't arise spontaneously and full-grown out of nowhere, and they're not the result of luck or clever marketing. They're based on science, research into the laws of human nature, and his efforts to satisfy needs that begged filling. They're the result of the events of his life, the influences he encountered, and the people who helped him grow.

This book is about how this man became the international influence he has been and will be for years to come.

Fans of his will enjoy the story and find valuable insights. Instructional and performance improvement people will find guidance for their work and the reasons that Bob's methods work so very well. Friends who were with him during various parts of the journey will enjoy connecting again with him and the story. Students will see how his ideas and approaches were born and grew, and learn some valuable lessons about being critical evaluators of what goes on around them. Those who aren't sure how to proceed with their careers, in whatever field, may well find inspiration. And no matter who you are, his insights and experiences will make you laugh out loud.

Besides all of that, it's a great read.

Seth N. Leibler, Ed.D.

Why Is This?

FEW PEOPLE SPRING FROM THE WOMB PRE-DESTINED TO BECOME RENOWNED GRAPE-PEELERS—OR ANYTHING ELSE. Few blossom forth with unshakable convictions about their destinations in life. Life, after all, is messy. The events that shape our lives don't always appear when we are ready to receive them. They don't stand in line to wait their turn. They appear from surprising directions and sources at unexpected times, and never arrive with road maps or operator's manuals.

Truth is, we seldom even become aware of our talents and aspirations until we experience some of life's offerings. It's after experimentation, after observing living exemplars and trying on possible personas, that we discover our talents and consider making selections from the vast occupational cafeteria. Even then, new experiences and insights steer us into different directions, often more than once.

In that sense, life *is* like a pinball machine. The ball shoots forward, and then, jostled by the thumps of bumpers and flippers, changes direction many times before finally dropping into the trough of eternity.

The analogy is flawed, of course; we are much more than inert little balls of steel. We need not passively accept the thumps and whacks of the bumpers and flippers of life; we can navigate according to our capabilities, motivations, aspirations, and dreams. Events can shoot us off in new directions, but we can shape the success or failure of those moves by our own determination and skill, or lack thereof. We can even influence the length of our journey (to some degree) before finally succumbing to the inevitable pull of time.

In other words, getting from there to here can be as much influenced by the talents and urges sprouting from our hereditary soup as by chance events and the people who star in them.

Why this book then? Many bumps and flips have led me from there to here—from the primordial ooze, so to speak, to the present day. I want to highlight the pings jostling me along life's pathways, and to note some of the lessons and insights influencing my choices.

It is also my intent to set the record straight. Over the years, I've been fortunate to have a number of people write about me, and though I am grateful for their attention, there have inevitably been a few inaccuracies published about myself and my work. I hope after strolling through this book, readers will be better able to decide for themselves. As Thomas Sowell put it, "I urge my fellow old-timers to write their memoirs, just so that 'revisionist historians' will not be able to get away with lying about the past."

But the motivation behind this work has deeper roots. I've often been asked various versions of, "Why did you decide to do that?" and, "How did you come to do what you do?" I've been asked often enough to warrant a more thoughtful reply than a quick, "It just happened," or "I just backed into it." So I've given it some thought, and within these pages, tried to answer.

Finally, no matter how long one has thrashed about on this planet, it may be useful to be reminded that current practices didn't spring from the void fully matured. Because I've been around since the Big Bang—Hannibal and I used to ski the Alps together—I feel qualified to comment on some of these practices. But this is neither a history nor a textbook; it is simply my narrative of the bumps and pings that have nudged me from there to here.

Like yours, my path has been shaped by people and events, as well as by aspirations, perceptions, and a lot of hard work. Some of the people I've had the privilege to know went out of their way to teach me something of how the world actually works. Those were encounters of vast utility. Maybe some of those insights will be useful to you too.

R. F. Mager
March, 2003

one

In the Dawn of Time . . .

IT WAS THE SUMMER OF 1923. Pterodactyls and brontosaurs roamed the countryside, terrorizing the peasants and fertilizing the land. It was a time of revelry and plenty—often referred to as the Roaring Twenties. Apparently, I was a result of one of the roars—whooshed right into the middle of that doomed age of prosperity.

People had everything then: horse-drawn milk- and ice-wagons, shiny new buggy whips and electric cars. They danced the Charleston and hoisted their glasses to the rising stock market. Automobiles chugged along the streets and an exciting new invention called radio was in its infancy. How infant? My father had a crystal set on which he listened to the Clarence Darrow debates, provided he could place the "cat's whisker" at just the right spot on the galena crystal to tune the station in. His most profound verbalization during these trying moments was "Shhh! Shhh!" accompanied by wild arm-waving.

By the time the stock market crashed in 1929, I was six. I grew to sixteen during the depth of the Depression. Though the ravages of those hard times were as yet of little interest to me—I was too busy dodging the bullies in the school yard—they made a lasting impression. I've never forgotten the stream of poor people coming to our door hoping to sell a pair of shoelaces or a pair of pencils for two or three pennies. Nor the despair in the faces of the long lines of the unemployed. These people were not bums—they were honest people put out of work as one result of the stock market crash. And we weren't rich. Ask anyone who lived through those trying times if they don't sometimes dread slipping back into poverty.

The Depression wasn't the only source of significant influence. Custom—and the law—required young urchins to attend public schools. You may think these consisted of a log with a teacher on one end and students piled on the other, but you'd be wrong—it wasn't *that* long ago. The schools may have been built to resemble brick egg-crates, but they managed to disgorge ragamops quite able to read, write, and spell—all without the aid of drugs and subsidized football teams.

The schools worked hard to impart the basic skills I would need to successfully navigate the communities in which I might live, and the occupations in which I might find myself engaged. Periodically, students were tagged with labels called "grades," usually based on some mystical variation of "the curve." Sometimes they were accompanied by explanations. I have evidence (in the form of exhumed report cards) testifying that my main "problem" was "not working up to my potential." I had no idea what that meant or what I was supposed to do about it, except work harder. That advice was as helpful as my father telling me to "Grow up already!" Such exhortations may have blown fuel into my motivational gas tank, but did nothing whatsoever to steer me in productive directions.

Even so, I plodded on and learned what I could. Of course, not all the learning was dispensed by the schools themselves. As you well know, insights that jostle your complacency can come from any direction. Once, when a friend and I were walking home from school, we observed a pair of older adults cavorting their way down the street.

When we laughed at this embarrassing display, the old gent leaned over and asked, "At what age are *you* going to want to stop having fun?" Ask yourself that question next time you see older people enjoying themselves.

Disaster struck at the end of the fourth grade, when it was decreed that I would skip Grade 5. I've never forgiven them for that. I became the smallest boy in the sixth grade, and was picked on with regularity. Worse were the gaps created in my knowledge. Being deprived of all the experiences my classmates had had in the fifth grade, I often didn't know what the other kids were talking about. That led to snickers, and sometimes jeers. I still haven't filled all the gaps. As I said, I'll never forgive them for that.

Still worse was the language gap. Apparently fifth graders learned about grammar and parsing. Endlessly, according to the victims. At the time, I smirked over not having to endure that "boring" material. Later, I wished I'd had the privilege of being bored with grammar along with everyone else (the parsing part has never been missed).

It was also common to burn at the stake anyone who dared to write with the left hand. It was considered a heinous act and often resulted in a sharp rap on the knuckles. Kicking and screaming, I switched to my right hand. That explains my inability to write legibly with either hand.

Even so, with the help of any number of dedicated teachers, I forged a few rudimentary swords with which to hack my way through life. I was a kid and had little concern about a career, except for the usual aspirations about firemen, policemen, detectives, cowboys and rocketship pilots. We kids pretended to be each of these, until we exhausted our meager knowledge of other options that might be available on the occupational landscape.

I even tinkered with music. I spent a lot of hours practicing, first the violin (my father played a gypsy violin), then the clarinet and sax. I even played in the high school symphony orchestra—for one whole week. Having been raised in an environment filled with rousing gypsy music, I found the steady stream of classical music boring. Worse, everybody in the violin section played the same thing, the same way, from the same piece of music. Hanging around those gypsy musicians, who wouldn't be caught dead playing anything the same way twice, had convinced me that "people who read music cheat." I decided it was time to escape. (I'm now married to a professional classical musician, so I'd better change the subject before she starts rustling the divorce papers.) Suffice to say, when I added a little gypsy embellishment to whatever classical ditty we were playing, it was made clear I should seek my fortune elsewhere. Somehow though, I think Mozart might have approved.

Though I tasted a wide variety of activities from birth through high school, not a glimmer of occupational direction had as yet appeared.

Little did I know the pinball flippers had already struck.

two

First Nudges

LET'S EXPLORE SOME OF THOSE PRODS. The first nudge bumped me one sunny morning when, as a small boy, I watched my father take apart the family car. All the way to the chassis. Small boys like the idea of taking things apart, and the thought of being able to disassemble something as large as an automobile was exciting. The idea was just destructive enough to make my eyeballs bulge. Though I was too young to understand it all, he nonetheless explained the function of each part as he placed it on the ground. After my "help" had been enlisted to clean the pieces, I watched him reassemble it as he told me again what each part did. When he was finished, he made it come to life.

It would be hard to convey the exhilaration caused by that event; to this day I rely on the mental image of how cars work learned from that hands-on experience. It wasn't formal instruction, it wasn't part of a course, and I wasn't working for a grade. But because I actually made tactile contact with the intriguing task, I paid close attention as the learning seeped into my muscles as well as my brain. I had no idea how important the hands-on habit would become.

Later, I realized the experience had had another effect on me. Though amazed to learn that my father could disassemble the family car, I was even more impressed to watch him put it back together—all by himself. Without the help of a committee, diagrams, or instructions, or even a grant from the government. Looking back, it was a dazzling display of the power of self-sufficiency. He held in his hands the skills with which to take the world by the muffler and make it do his bidding.

From that sunny day on, it became my quest to take apart as many things as possible (he said, grinning gleefully). Even today, I still feel great joy whenever, through the power of my own skills, I make a faucet stop leaking or the VCR start working—while saving a basket of dollars in the process. But even from the beginning, something more than joy accompanied the take-apart and put-together sessions. Through these early sessions, I began learning to observe and gradually see what was actually there to be seen.

The nudge toward an analytical mindset would become enormously useful much later when I was faced with the mushy world of abstractions—e.g., be enthusiastic, listen accurately, develop a feel for economics, value freedom. It came as something of a shock to realize that these, and thousands of utterances like them, were little more than verbal smoke—the result of fuzzy-mindedness masquerading as clarity and substance. Useful for dazzling the readers of the corporate annual report, perhaps, but useless for describing the human behavior they purported to characterize. These verbal emperors were more than a little naked. Later in life I would turn my attention to exposing them for the obfuscators they were.

Hobnobbing with the dead

A pinball bumper nudged me again—pong!—during my junior high years when my father took me to visit a friend who worked at the Cleveland city morgue. Significantly, he didn't make an issue of it.

That we would be in the presence of dead bodies wasn't accompanied by expressions of fear or loathing, or with attempts to demonize the experience—the body-filled landscape was simply taken for granted.

The morgue technician casually explained that the strange smell was formaldehyde, a smell I've recognized ever since. As we walked down the line of partially-covered corpses, I remember being surprised by the toe-tags. That seemed a callous way to treat a human being, and I said so. In response, the technician explained that it was actually a compassionate way to treat the dead. The practice helped prevent errors in the disposition of the bodies (such as sending a white body to be viewed by a black grieving family, or vice versa). I'd leaped from a toe-tag to a wrong conclusion and was glad to be set straight.

When asked whether I wanted to touch one of the bodies, I said "Sure." I wasn't sure at all, but didn't feel I could back out when the kindly dead-keeper was being so helpful. So I did, and learned what the skin of a recently-dead body feels like. Cold, mostly. I also learned the dead don't bite.

I'd seen bodies before, of course, but those were all displayed in coffins, like clothed salamis arranged on satin doilies. As a child, there were numerous "opportunities" to observe women collecting at the funeral parlor to weep while the men slipped across the street to the saloon. (That seemed right to me, though I wasn't allowed into the saloon except to buy a five-cent pitcher of beer to take home to Dad.) Unfortunately, the frequent visits to church and funeral parlor caused me to associate church—and the smell of flowers—with death.

I didn't know it at the time, but these experiences helped prepare me for the more gruesome sights of war. The morgue revelations also provided another lesson about how the world worked. "Have you ever thought about where bodies go when they die?" the corpse-caretaker asked. No, I hadn't thought about that. I hadn't thought about any of the infrastructure of life—about what made communities work, and about the people who turned the cranks, gruesome or otherwise. I hadn't thought about such things until then. From then on, I began watching people at work. By the time my Army days began, the presence of death had lost most of its dread, and the seed of curiosity about how things worked—and who did what—had been planted.

Dipping a toe

That curiosity was stroked and fanned during summer jobs in the real world. Between high school and college I spent an exciting summer working as a technician for Ma Bell. The job involved connecting and disconnecting telephone lines in a central office and clearing troubles. Trouble-clearing was a race against time. Brandishing a hot soldering iron, we dashed madly up and down the floor-to-ceiling frames on rolling ladders, trying desperately to clear a trouble before the time limit expired. The work suited me and I had the time of my life. But at the end of the summer it was time to march toward college, and so I left that exciting job—with a great deal of reluctance. I had had no idea the world of work could be such fun.

The following summer (1942), I found a job in a factory that manufactured turret lathes, among other things. (These are machines used to make parts for other machines.) My job was to tap holes and screw little nameplates onto the turret lathe chassis. I wasn't there a week, however, before a union steward sidled up to me to announce, "You've got thirty days to join the union." Or else! Zheesh. I wasn't happy about union rules dictating the skimpy number of nameplates I could screw onto a lathe bed per hour—especially when any of us could have been 4-5 times as productive without raising a sweat. So at the end of the thirty-day period I took the "or else" and moved on.

I next found myself on the assembly line of a factory manufacturing submarine motors for the Navy. The work was vital to the war effort, but wasn't too thrilling. Fortunately, it wasn't all routine. Frustrating, but not routine. One step in the assembly process involved inserting a bakelite insulator into the motor housing. Trouble was, the bakelite inserts were brittle and frequently cracked when we bent them to fit the curvature of the housing. So we tried heating them. That worked—sometimes. Provided we didn't heat them to the point of melting. We scrapped a lot of bakelite. That episode taught me there was room for ingenuity even on an assembly line.

Somewhere along the way, I found myself at General Electric with the job title of Assistant District Statistician. Sounds pretty hot, doesn't it? In fact, my job was to update the sales books of the sales staff. Every month. Put another row of numbers in the columns, draw another dot on the graphs. Boring! One day it was discovered I'd lost one whole entire submarine—in my reports. By accident, you understand. Though I enjoyed playing in the GE band at the summer picnic, it was time to move on.

The reason for mentioning this melange of summer jobs is that each drilled the importance of education deeper into my skull. Yes, I now realized, there were fun jobs in the world, and jobs that paid pretty well (there was a war on, remember). Without more education, however, my life choices would be constrained by my limited quiver of skills. Not wanting to limp through life with fewer skills than I was able to absorb, I looked forward to returning to the campus each fall with renewed determination—to study, that is. Education was the magic key to expanding control over my own destiny.

That worked pretty well until the summer of 1943, when life took a decidedly different turn.

three

Uncle Sam Wants Me?

I HAD ENTERED COLLEGE IN THE FALL OF 1941. College provided a rich supply of bumps and flips; almost every course aroused interest and propelled me in a different direction. I was like a kid in a candy store, wanting first to become one of these, then one of those, the constant stream of revelations and new knowledge turning me 'round and 'round. At the time, I thought I could be happy doing that forever. Some kindly advisor had told me to "Do *something*" when faced with uncertainties regarding life choices. "By doing *something*," he'd said, "you'll gain experience and be ready when opportunities arise—even though you may soon be doing something else." That was good advice. So I settled on psychology as my initial focus.

Even so, the subject of logic was so fascinating I briefly entertained the notion of becoming a philosopher. That passion grew dim, however, when I couldn't see myself wearing a beard. Looking back at all the instructing I've done, it seems odd I never once fantasized about becoming a teacher.

Everything went well enough that freshman fall of 1941—until December 7 brought the explosive announcement of the attack on Pearl Harbor. That got everyone's attention and emotions ran high. Those of us with pistols in our closets made sure they were well oiled. What we planned to do with .22 caliber pistols in the event of an attack on the campus wasn't clear, but we were ready.

Some of us had enrolled in ROTC (Reserve Officers Training Corps) that fall of 1941, to learn something about the art of war. That training turned out to be extremely useful, and, as an added benefit, bought temporary deferral from the draft.

In the summer of 1943, however, Uncle Sam sent an urgent appeal for my services. He was conducting an enterprise called World War II and was in desperate need of my personal assistance. If I would just help him win the war he would pay me the princely sum of twenty-one dollars each and every month. How could I refuse? In addition to the big salary, he promised to send me back to college to complete a degree before sending me off to OCS (Officer Candidate School) at Fort Benning, Georgia. He lied.

I received the draft notice in early summer of 1943 and went to Fort Hayes, Columbus, Ohio, for processing—aptitude and intelligence testing, health checkup by Doctor U. Bendover, uniforms and other gear. From there we were put on a train headed west, as the Basic Training extravaganza was scheduled to occur in the dusty desert at Camp Fannin, Texas.

Until then, I had never met or interacted with the "barely functional" fraction of the population, and was surprised to learn of its existence. But, as the draft netted a cross-section of humanity—with everything that implied—we had to find ways to protect ourselves from these potentially lethal people (they are *not* the folks you want near you in a combat situation).

I was astonished to discover during Basic Training that not everyone knew their left foot from their right, or could learn to disassemble a simple rifle, or had enough sense not to blind themselves by drinking hair tonic. When I was assigned to drill a squad riddled with these misfits, I cringed with frustration whenever they tripped over their own feet or inadvertently clubbed their neighbor with the rifle they couldn't learn to control. (Much later, when I was grumbling about being surrounded by incompetents, a kindly soul took the time to offer some perspective. "Y'know," he said, "no matter your intelligence level, you're just going to have to learn to make room in this world for those less fortunate." That was a major whack upside the head. I hadn't thought about it that way.

One day I made the mistake of speaking out about what I, and other members of my company, considered unnecessary cruelty from our drill sergeant. That evening, the drill sergeant invited me to join him behind the latrine. Uh-oh, I thought, he's going to beat the tar out of me . . . he's miffed about my smart remarks and is going to teach me a lesson. I was sure of it.

He did, but not the one I expected. Calmly and deliberately he explained the facts of life relating to the difficulty of turning soft, peace-loving civilians into soldiers. He explained his responsibility in giving these innocents the skills and attitudes they'd need if they expected to stay alive. In other words, it was his job to play a life-and-death role in the theater of life. It was a most unexpected lecture, delivered like a kindly professor confiding the secrets of love to his belligerent son. Needless to say, those shared confidences changed my attitude about drill sergeants and the hardships they made us endure.

When Basic Training ended after thirteen weeks, the plan was to climb onto a train chugging to a Midwest university where we would complete our undergraduate education before heading for OCS. But a funny thing happened on the way to the war. True, we headed for the train platform—at the last minute, however, another soldier and I were kept behind. Cruel and unusual punishment, we thought. Like rejected lovers, we stood on the platform waving goodbye as our comrades in arms chugged into the distance.

Abandoned to the scrap heap of life, we gnawed on possible causes.

Why weren't we allowed on the train? Had alleged misdeeds finally caught up with us? Had we left our bunks too limp? No, it turned out we were held back to become part of the cadre (instructors) assigned to train new batches of recruits. Why were we singled out for this honor? Because we were the two best marksmen in the battalion. Their reasoning was, as "everybody knows," he who shoots straightest will automatically make a fine instructor. Stop laughing. The experience provided important insights about how military management (there are those who consider that an oxymoron) worked. The fateful pinball flipper had given me its first whack toward the direction of a career in learning and performance, but I was still a long way from caring.

After a few months in which we managed to teach new recruits the important secrets of war, such as how to fill a canteen from a Lister bag (think water-filled punching bag with nipples), a few other instructors and I were shipped to Camp Blanding, the sand flea capital of Florida. There, we were to serve as cadre for a new anti-tank training battalion. Anti-tank? What's that? None of the sergeants nor I, by now a full-fledged corporal, knew anything about tanks or anti-tanks. But we had experience with training infantry, so we were expected to know how to train anti-tankers. Sound familiar?

While milling around one day wondering how to organize ourselves for the imminent arrival of the first recruits, we shared information about our personal backgrounds. When I let slip that I could type with one finger of each hand—presto, I became the company clerk. It followed, right? If he can type with two fingers, he obviously has the clerical skills needed for the job. (Actually, this turned out to be a lucky break; it exempted me from the joys of crawling among the sand fleas. It also bestowed upon me some power and influence: I became the keeper of the key to the Coke machine, as well as dispenser of the cold beer I kept in its secret compartment.)

From the streets of New York

Our mission as an anti-tank training battalion was to process arriving groups of peace-loving recruits and turn them into trained soldiers willing to pull the trigger of a loaded weapon. Can you imagine how hard that is? Most people can't even *imagine* pulling a trigger in anger—until, that is, somebody starts shooting at them or their loved ones.

Shortly after our milling-around period, we received a rag-tag bag of civilians fresh from the streets of New York. These were good, solid citizens yanked from their working lives and sent to this alien planet to learn things they'd rather not know. When they arrived, they were marched into the Company area and made to stand at attention while the company commander told them how to behave, and about the dire consequences to follow if they didn't. One of the recruits, a family man about thirty-five years old, broke down during this speech and began to sob, completely overwhelmed.

This being a formal formation, I stood at parade rest along with the other non-coms while Captain Insensitive ignored the distressed "soldier" and continued barking. It wasn't long before I boiled over and strode to the soldier, gently took his rifle, and escorted him to the nearest barrack. We sat across from one another on a pair of bunks and just chatted. I recalled a technique I'd learned during a college therapy course, and began to ask him about his wife and kids, and what he did for a living. Within ten minutes he was ready to return to the formation, after which he had no problem with the transition to Army life.

Surprisingly, nobody complained about my breaking ranks without permission. Later, I suspected the officers were secretly relieved that someone took charge of an embarrassing situation. It was becoming clear that *doing* leads to fewer negative consequences than *asking for permission*, an insight that would be enormously useful in the years to follow.

Enter the publisher

During the days that followed, I realized the problems experienced by new recruits were created mainly by the absence of information: Nobody bothered to explain the basic rules of the game. It wasn't that they weren't told what to *do*—they were constantly given orders about what to do and how to behave. The problem was that they were seldom told *why*. Gee, I wondered, would it hurt the military establishment to explain the reasons for keeping weapons squeaky clean, the reasons for enduring long marches with heavy packs, for keeping mind and body in good health? Apparently it would; the mission was to teach recruits to follow orders without thinking or asking for explanations.

Something needed to be done. Again, without asking permission, I wrote a little booklet explaining how things worked, along with a few words of explanation . . . the lay of the land, so to speak.

I went into town the following weekend and paid forty dollars for a hand-cranked A.B. Dick Mimeograph machine. With it, I printed enough booklets to give to our Company A recruits. Though I'm not a cartoonist, I drew a cover-cartoon and included a few corny couplets to lighten the tone.

I showed my masterpiece to the first sergeant, who told me to distribute copies to the recruits. By the following day, the battalion commander had learned about the event (first sergeants operate a grapevine so efficient it puts the speed of light to shame). I could see myself heading for the stockade for distributing illicit material. But no! He'd called me into his office to ask if I'd mind if he distributed additional copies to the other three companies. Can you imagine a major asking a corporal for permission? Naturally, I agreed. They printed it exactly as they received it, including the cartoon cover specifically addressing the contents to the soldiers of Company A. (I still chuckle over what the soldiers of Companies B, C, and D must have thought about that.)

The pinball bumper had given me another nudge toward a career in learning and performance. I still didn't know much about how to teach or about how students learned, and I didn't yet aspire in that direction. I just saw a need and tried to fill it. I was, however, becoming somewhat adept at recognizing instances where people were hurting from lack of information.

Inching closer

Obviously, I was doing such a great job as a company clerk it was a cinch I'd be even more successful as a combat infantryman. I soon found myself reassigned and lounging on the Queen Elizabeth cruising toward Glasgow. (If you believe that "lounging" part, I've got a bridge . . .) We completed the journey without being torpedoed, and choo-chooed to the embarkation port in the south of England. Thus it was that twenty-eight days after D-Day (June 6, 1944), I found myself on the Cherbourg Peninsula trudging up Utah Beach toward the shooting war. I was twenty-one years old.

After sloshing about in the mud dodging bullets and other debris for a couple of months, I was slightly wounded (it only hurt when I tried to sit) and evacuated to a field hospital set up on the grounds of a large chateau near Cherbourg. When I recovered, the hospital staff insisted I was fit for duty and sent me trudging back toward my outfit at the front. Having by then discovered that getting shot at was a very risky occupation, I decided to try to find another job. Surely someone needed a soldier who could type with two fingers. I began knocking on the doors of every personnel office at every replacement depot I bunked at along the way.

"Please, sir, I'd be much better at any number of things than shooting at the enemy. I can even type with two fingers. Are you *sure* you don't have any openings?"

No luck, and after each rejection I inched closer and closer to the shooting war. But I was determined to find greener—and less muddy—pastures. Then, behind the door of the personnel office of the last replacement depot on my journey, I found an old buddy from college sitting behind the desk.

Just as I was about to drop to my knees to plead for a job, he said,

"Boy, am I glad you're here. We've got something going and we're having trouble staffing it."

The expression "music to my ears" probably came to mind. Another thwack upside the head.

"I'm your man," I replied, not trying to hide my eagerness. "What's the job?"

"I'm not sure," he said. "There's a new unit being formed, called I&E . . . Information/Education."

"I'll take it," I said. "What's it about?"

"Well, we'll have you assigned here and you'll brief the transient troops on current events. Everybody wants to see updated maps showing where their units are located. Mostly, though, they just want to know when they'll be going home."

"That's the information part. What about the education part?"

"I dunno. Maybe you can dream something up."

He had me assigned to the depot and gave me a private office the size of a barn. Thus began my career as an Information/Education guy—whatever that was.

Nobody knew what I&E guys were supposed to do, so I found myself with time on my hands. My passion at that time was radio, so I amused myself collecting liberated Telefunken radio equipment and puttering with it during odd moments. I didn't know how to make it do anything, though, as I'd had no training in electronics. So I just stared at it and practiced taking it apart.

One day, the commander of the replacement depot appeared in my office, and a comedy worthy of the Marx Brothers followed.

"I want you to set up a public address system out in that field so I can address the troops." He pointed to the field.

"But sir, I don't know how to do that."

"Don't argue with me, soldier. That's an order!"

Those with military experience know this is not an unusual dialogue between colonels and corporals. Repeated protestations of ignorance had no effect. So what could I do? With visions of the doom soon to follow, I dragged some of my Telefunken hardware to the edge of the field where the troops had already assembled. Embarrassed, I placed it on a table and tinkered, pretending to set it up.

When nothing happened, the Colonel shouted disparaging remarks in my direction. Those didn't make the equipment work either. The troops grew restless, and the colonel continued his stream of invective.

While my head was bent in concentration, I heard a voice say, "Can I help?" Looking up, I saw a short, thin master sergeant with graying hair holding a worn metal eyeglass case in his hand.

"The Colonel insisted I bring this stuff down here, but I don't have any idea how to make it work," I said.

"Let me take a look." He opened his eyeglass case and extracted a small tool—I think it was a tiny magic wand. He bent to his work, and within seconds the PA system came to life. The Colonel addressed the troops and the day was saved.

My immediate response was to have this wizard sergeant assigned as my assistant; his task would be to teach me something about electronics. He was delighted—and why not? He was perfectly happy to avoid the conflagration in the Pacific.

So we began. This gentle and patient man—Staff Sergeant Carl Knelly—a designer of whole, entire radio stations in civilian life, taught me about electronics. First he had me learn to rewind a voice coil for a two-inch loudspeaker. He "forgot" to tell me this was an extremely delicate task, so I simply kept at it until I succeeded.

I've often thought of that experience, especially when listening to a teacher tell me that students must be spoon-fed words commensurate with their age and grade level. Think about that next time you see a young child singing—and spelling—words like supercalifragilisticexpialidocious. Think about it next time you wonder where your kids learned things they shouldn't know until much older.

Little by little, my patient tutor showed me how to perform simple tasks while explaining the theory behind them. Notice the sequence.

First he showed me the task, then I performed the task, and finally he revealed something of the theory associated with it. It was one of those unexpected life events that had no particular significance until later. Without realizing it, the sergeant modeled exemplary instructional behavior, and I benefited from it.

It wasn't my fault

My growing skill with things electronic led to mischief. Think: Revenge of the Nerd.

Once I'd actually learned to make the equipment work like a PA system (without being rescued), I had loudspeakers mounted on a tall telephone pole at the edge of the "parade ground." This allowed me to play music for the bored troops. Naturally, this led to another visit from the Colonel.

"You will play march music for Retreat," he barked. For the uninitiated, Retreat is a formation that occurs late in the afternoon—sort of an end-of-day stroll around the parade ground. In our case, a grassy field.

"But Colonel, I don't have any march music."

"You *will* play march music for Retreat."

"All I have is a couple of captured Nazi goose-stepping marches."

Now that the war had been over for a couple of weeks, the rear-echelon desk jockeys' (i.e., bureaucrats who had never experienced real combat) spit-n-polish obsessions began creeping like a cancer into our daily lives. "I don't care *what* they are. Play marches."

When pushed too far, even a mouse will turn and roar. That afternoon, I played Nazi march music while the troops tried to avoid goose-stepping to the beat. Then, an evil grin spreading across my face, I segued from the march into a rumba (I had two turntables).

Pandemonium followed. The soldiers tangled themselves in their own feet as they tried to match the cadence of the rumba. They stumbled into one another. When they realized what was happening, they began to chuckle. After that they simply stopped the marching and hip-wiggling to make it easier to double over with laughter.

By then the Colonel was in full flight across the parade ground toward my open office window.

"Stop it! Stop it!" he shrieked.

But I couldn't stop it, could I? I pretended to try to make it stop, of course, but I was laughing so hard it was difficult to wrap my fingers around the volume control. Surely you understand.

Needless to say, I earned a lot of hero points that day. The troops snickered over that incident for weeks, and to this day I don't know where I found the balls to do that. But I'm glad I did. (The reason the Colonel didn't flay me alive will be obvious to any old soldier. Rear-echelon officers—those doing their deeds far behind the front lines—usually walked a bit gingerly among fresh-from-the-foxhole combat troops still carrying guns.)

Across the Atlantic in a tin can

Several months later I'd earned enough points to join the stream of happy folk returning to the United States. After out-processing— stripping us of our weapons, etc.—we boarded a Liberty Ship for the trip home. Because a lot of shipping was required to serve the war effort, Liberty Ships had been manufactured like jelly beans. They were small ships, quickly built and sparsely furnished. Troops (landlubbers) were bunked below, each in his own entire individual hammock.

Our return trip took us through the worst winter storm of the North Atlantic. It was so severe, the flight deck of the aircraft carrier Wasp, sailing through the same storm, was smashed by the waves. That wasn't easy—even in 1945, flight decks were built high above the water.

Imagine a shipload of troops bouncing around in a tin can. The prow of the ship reached toward the sky as it tried rising over a wave, and then shuddered as it plunged into the trough that followed. Over and over. We wondered when—not if—the ship would break apart. We learned later the crew was ordered to lock the hatches to prevent our appearing on deck; only seasoned sailors had the skill with which to keep from being blown overboard.

My hammock hung in the prow, that part of the ship rising the highest under the waves and dropping farthest when they passed. Thinking I might avoid getting sick if my mind were focused on something else, I rummaged through my duffle bag for a book. *Tropic of Cancer*, or perhaps *Lady Chatterley's Lover*, would have been nice. Alas, the only book I could find was called, *How to Think Straight*, by Robert H. Thouless. What? A book on logic? I was hoping for something a little more engrossing. But Thouless was all I had, so I tried focusing on the words and ideas. For several days I studied that little pocket book—it's here before me as I write—and I credit it with saving me from the seasickness to which many others succumbed. At the same time, it taught me more about logic than I'd learned in college.

Several days later the Statue of Liberty blossomed into view. It was a beautiful sight.

four

Appearances Can Deceive

URING THE NEXT FEW YEARS I bumped into people and events that poked holes in the boundaries of my personal box, broadened my horizons, and rubbed my nose in facts of life I might have preferred doing without. By the time I returned to Ohio University in the fall of 1946, I'd been nudged away from a career in psychology toward a life in radio. But because I was so close, I decided to continue work on the psychology degree while diving into speech and theater courses.

I also worked at the campus radio station, discovering that broadcasting was rich with fun and challenge. On the technical side, I helped keep the equipment running and expanded the reach of the station's limp signal by running antenna wires through the university steam tunnels. On the artistic side, I met and mingled with the "talent"—singers, musicians, actors, professors—appearing on the programs. Before long, I became an announcer, and that led to another whack by the flippers of life.

Catch 22

You'll find this familiar—you can't get a job without experience (or connections), and you can't get experience without a job. That was as true in radio as in other areas. It was a stroke of luck, therefore, when an opportunity presented itself—a job, and therefore experience, in commercial broadcasting. An older student had decided to enroll in college after a successful career as a radio/television announcer at a Columbus, Ohio station. Before the end of his first semester, though, he was offered a job as manager of a radio station in central Tennessee (the trotting horse center of the world). He knew my work, and, probably because we got along well together, asked me to join him as a staff announcer. He also asked me to fill in as program director, a job about which I knew nothing.

One small hitch. To avail myself of the opportunity, I'd have to leave college—just one semester short of graduation. It was a difficult decision requiring much thought and consultation with friends and faculty. In the end, it came to this: I could always re-enroll in college, but I couldn't be sure of another opportunity like this one. Logic favored taking the job. How could I not? It was my ticket *in*.

Lessons from a small town

After moving to a rooming-house, I settled into the routine. Drag out of bed at 3 a.m. and stagger to an all-night diner for breakfast. Head for the radio station, where the Gospel Trio waited on the steps, eager to open the broadcasting day at 4 a.m.!

I thought 4 a.m. was an uncivilized hour to put a station on the air, and one morning made the mistake of saying so—into an open microphone. The switchboard lit up with farmers calling to tell me, "Sonny, by the time you crank up that station I already done most of my chores." They were right to put me in my place; I never made that mistake again. It was another eye-opening lesson in how the world worked. Who would have thought people were awake—and working—at that hour of the night?

Another mistake I made only once was to forget to announce the egg prices along with the hog and cattle prices. Farmers' wives depended on egg money for their livelihood and rained woe on any announcer who forgot to keep them informed of current prices. These humbling thumps served as reminders that the world wasn't about me, and that I'd best pay closer attention to the roles others played in making the world turn.

Radio evangelists

Small-station announcers announce all kinds of programs, including those of the radio evangelists. These assignments often provided a jaundiced-eye view of the spiritual—the view from behind the altar was always different from that seen from the pew. I was unprepared for the advanced education I was about to receive. It began with my first radio job and continued through those that followed.

At the first station, for example, an evangelist arrived to preach for half an hour twice a week. Each week the same scenario would unfold. I'd remind him that the microphone was sensitive, and therefore he should stand a foot away from it when speaking. Then I'd remind him that I'd hold up five fingers when he had five minutes of air time remaining, and so on.

When I turned on his microphone, though, he would ram his nose against it and begin shouting. He would remove his tie, and then his jacket. While undressing, he would overload the microphone so badly it was almost impossible to understand a word he said.

When five minutes remained, I would calmly hold up five fingers, at which point he would stop shouting, and in mid-sentence say, ". . . Well, I guess they want me to get out of here." Gathering his clothing, he then would leave the studio.

The first time that happened I was frantic: how could I fill those five minutes of dead air? Desperation often inspiring invention, I soon solved the problem. From then on, whenever he left me with dead air, I announced, "Reverend _____ has asked me to summarize his sermon," after which I made something up. You wouldn't believe what's in the Bible. The astonishing thing was that not one person called to complain about my "summaries." Instead, at least one nice lady called to tell me how much she appreciated my clearly-spoken Bible messages.

When I took a job at another station in a nearby state, we had a preacher who delivered a weekly afternoon sermon. As he did so, his attractive sixteen-year-old daughter sat in the control room with me, gleefully telling me the details about all the boys she was sleeping with—just to get even with her strict and "evil" father.

Later, I moved to a station in Texas. This happened to be during the Texas City disaster in 1948 when several oil storage tanks exploded. One day, a preacher and three of his congregation showed up at the studio with a check for sixty dollars. Many announcers had established disaster funds, and the preacher's task was to hand me the check representing the congregation's offerings. When they turned to leave, one of the three gentlemen accompanying the preacher whispered that they were present mainly to make sure the preacher did, in fact, hand over the money.

Later still, during a radio job in Norfolk, Virginia, my education about broadcast religion continued. I worked the early morning shift—including Sunday. At this station, business customers were billed for air time at the end of the month; religionists, on the other hand, were required to pay in advance. That, according to the station manager, was because they couldn't be trusted to pay their bills. Management required that I demand payment before allowing these nice folks on the air. I found that immensely embarrassing. Nonetheless, when one or another group arrived with a paper bag containing nickels and dimes, we counted them out together on one of the control room turntables. Fortunately, I never had to turn anyone away and so never had to ad lib more Bible stories.

There was a bright spot. At the Tennessee station we enjoyed the companionship of a preacher so reliable and trustworthy we felt safe installing a pre-amplifier in the basement of his church. He would contact us for a time-check just before his broadcast, start his program exactly on time, and end exactly on time. That was a rare talent, as many believed the microphone should be left on as long as they wanted because they were spreading the word of God. We loved that man.

One day he came to the station to announce he was leaving town. When we asked why, he said, "Well, my congregation gave me a brand-new two-toned Chevrolet for my birthday, which I had to park in the street. When that big storm hit last week, it toppled a huge elm tree right onto my brand new car, folding it up like an accordion. I figured God was trying to tell me something, so I'm going to move to Florida." Which he did, and bought a radio station.

He was sorely missed.

Deadline-intensive occupations (like the broadcast media and newspapers) require reliability, plain and simple. If you can't be counted on to be there when you're due, don't apply . . . no matter how talented you may be. In other words, if you aren't reliable, you're nothing. Having developed the habit of starting and ending programs exactly on time—to the second—I am still intolerant of those who don't show up when and where they're expected. As you can guess, this causes friction when mingling with those for whom eight o'clock means "plus or minus thirty minutes." Aaarrrgh!

"Rasslers" du jour

During this string of radio jobs I was introduced to the world of professional wrestling, where more surprises lurked. One station sponsored an annual evening of such entertainment in the town square. To make it work, we rented the ring and associated equipment from the local Catholic priest—he owned it all—and called a rent-a-wrestler agency in a nearby city to hire a passle of talent. When the male and female wrestlers arrived—referee included as part of the package—we went to their hotel room to work out the scenario. My presence was required because, as the designated ring announcer, I had a part to play in the action-packed drama.

As the wrestlers and referee talked through their scenarios and coached me in my part, I must have sat like a dolt with my mouth open. I had no idea how carefully orchestrated and rehearsed these events were and was excited to become part of this entirely new world. Because it was the bad guy's turn to win, I was instructed to make sure a police officer would stand in his corner to escort him safely back to the hotel. The gullible get excited and tend to throw things when the bad guy wins.

I learned that not only was professional wrestling another manifestation of show business, but that professional wrestlers tended to be affable college graduates. Further, they took great pains not to hurt each other while plying their art. And yes, it was an art. (If you heard of a wrestler called "Killer So-and-so," it was probably because he/she accidentally hurt an opponent through carelessness or lack of skill.)

I never imagined I'd have an opportunity to peek behind the scenes of what is usually portrayed as a violent "sport," and certainly never imagined being asked to participate—even in a minor role—in the drama itself. To that point in my life, I had been a shy person, lacking in self-confidence. This defect, I believe, grew from early experiences. My father, the perfectionist—as a top-notch tool-and-die maker he had to be—was a source of constant correction. No matter what I did, he always responded by telling me how I might have done it better. He was right, of course, but I interpreted the constant barrage of "corrections" as put-downs, and gradually came to believe that nothing I did would ever be good enough. That heavy burden took a long time to shake off.

Too, with the exception of weekly poetry recitations in an eighth-grade English class, and a music recital or three, I had never performed in public. A fearless public speaker I was not. (Experience in front of a microphone didn't count; trained announcers realize they're not speaking to "the multitudes out there" but rather to a single individual listening to his/her radio in a relatively intimate setting. By the way, to teach novices to think of their audience as a single person, it often helps to drape a wig on their microphone.)

But when I stepped into the ring that evening and listened to the roar of the crowd, something wonderful happened. I came to life, squared my shoulders, and spread my arms in a wide gesture while introducing the event and the participants. The evening went as planned and the audience loved the show. After that, I had no difficulty speaking to audiences of any size. I had learned the secret of success—preparation and rehearsal. That evening, my self-image strengthened and my fear of new speaking situations changed to eagerness.

Pranks a lot

Radio stations—especially smaller ones—are breeding grounds for pranks. Announcers delight in breaking up their colleagues while they're on the air in front of a live microphone. It can be somewhat distracting to have someone light fire to your script—or remove your clothing—while you're reading the news. Self-control is a must-have.

One of our colleagues looked up one day to discover that the door to his announce booth had somehow come off its hinges and was floating down the hall. He completely collapsed in laughter. (The skulldugger held the door on his back as he bent over and crept past the booth window.) Not nice.

The event that branded the target as a prank magnet, however, happened the day he was doing a live on-the-street interview of a little girl returning from a wedding rehearsal. A word of warning: live on-the-street "anythings" are fraught with danger. When he asked the girl when the wedding was going to be, she replied, "They called it off."

At that point, warning bells should have sounded and he should have changed the subject or terminated the interview, but our fresh-from-college announcer plunged on. "Why was it called off?" he asked, falling into the pit of doom.

"Because she couldn't pass the blood test!" replied the girl. Moments later, his mike was cut off, after which he received a lesson from the station manager about facts of life on the street.

From then on, he was a marked man. One day, some anonymous person slipped into the announce booth, removed his shoes and socks (what could he do—he was on the air?) and slid a block of ice under his bare feet.

Ultimately, he learned, as did we all, to ignore such attacks and focus on our work without giggling or guffawing. I didn't realize until much later how valuable that practice would be.

Sounding off

The radio experience opened another exciting door, one that almost shoved me into an entirely new direction. With experience in commercial radio I was now qualified to apply for attendance at the 1947 summer NYU radio-television workshop. Because of the origin of the faculty, this was known locally as "CBS School." My application was accepted, so I headed for a summer in Greenwich Village and rented a third-floor walk-up. My rent was four dollars a month.

The workshop consisted of an intensive three-month curriculum during which everyone practiced all the functions—announcing, acting, writing, directing, and sound effects. Because television was in its infancy and growing fast, and because the workshop was billed as a radio/television workshop, we even received instruction in stage fencing (real fencing calls for minimum movement of the weapon; stage fencing involves maximum slashing and thrashing—ineffective for killing, but much more dramatic). It was stimulating to work with radio people from around the country, and learn from experienced network old-timers like announcer Howard Cheney and best-selling mystery writer Larry Mencken (no relation to H.L.)

Mencken, a large man, dripped practical information with every utterance.

"Don't ever, *ever*," he railed, "try to sell a network executive a script unless you've covered it with a two-paragraph explanation of how great it is and how wonderful it will be for the network. Why? Because not one of them can *see* or *hear* the story on your pages! They're bureaucrats, not artists. So you've got to tell them . . . and be sure to use itty-bitty words to do it." I've paraphrased, but that was the message.

My big insight that summer was learning of my natural talent for sound effects. Once I discovered that wonderful world, I thrived on sound effects, dreamed about them, and experimented with new sounds during every spare moment. It was a new and whimsical world. Had I finally discovered what I wanted to be when I grew up? Had I finally arrived at "Here"? Nothing I'd done to that point had been as interesting, exciting, exacting, and satisfying as sound effects. The exhilaration I experienced when operating five turntables and producing two simultaneous sets of footsteps was giddying. What more could life have to offer? After a few exploratory conversations with network sound men, however, I learned there was a downside to the craft: creeping poverty.

Alas, it was time to move on.

five

Into the Unknown

THE SAME YEAR (1948), I LEAPED simultaneously into two unknowns. The first was called matrimony, followed by the second—aimless travel. After twice marrying a young lady named Jeanne—once in secret and once six months later to satisfy parental expectations of the day—we packed the car and headed west. With no destination in mind, we just drove and sampled the countryside. Our unscripted journey took us to Tyler, Texas, where we decided to stay awhile. After renting an apartment and following earlier advice to *do something* when unsure of the next goal, I enrolled in Tyler Commercial College (TCC) to earn my amateur and commercial radio engineering licenses. Jeanne began teaching bookkeeping in the same institution.

Our meager income was augmented by part-time work at the local radio stations and earnings from recordings I made on the equipment purchased with my mustering-out money. It wasn't long before TCC called on my announcing experience, and I began teaching engineering students broadcasting techniques (announcing and control room operation). That added another pittance to the money pot.

Then a bizarre event unfolded.

He was dead serious

It began with a rap on the glass door to the studio. This was a bit annoying, as students had just started recording the commercials they'd been practicing. I could see through the glass door that the rapper was the school's chief engineer, so I stepped out to the hall to learn what he wanted. He introduced the visitor standing by his side.

"I understand you have a recording business," the man said.

"Yes, I do," I replied, dollar signs dancing before my eyes.

"I want you to record my funeral," the man said—deadpan.

My mind raced. I wasn't prepared for an assignment like that—I'd never even *heard* of an assignment like that. Was he serious? When was he planning to die? What does one wear when recording funerals? What will the minister say when I tell him I'll be placing microphones around the casket? This and more flashed through my mind in the second or two it took to regain my composure.

"All right," I replied, also deadpan. "When is it going to be?" I couldn't believe I was having this conversation.

"This afternoon," he said.

Jeezus, I thought, *this guy is serious*. After further discussion, the real story emerged. It wasn't *his* funeral we were talking about, but the funeral of a niece. He explained that it happened when his sister took his twelve-year-old niece to Dallas for her church confirmation. On the way, the sister turned the car over and the little girl burned to death in the resulting fire. The sister now lay in a Dallas hospital, and the man wanted the recording to play for the sister—so she wouldn't miss the funeral!

We worked out the financial details, and I went home to tell my wife.

"What are you doing home so early?" she asked.

"Oh," I replied casually, "I've got to record a funeral this afternoon."

Now it was her turn to be taken aback, after which we talked about what I should wear. We settled on a dark suit and black everything else.

As I drove to the funeral home, I became apprehensive about what the minister would say about the service being recorded. I needn't have worried. The Baptist minister was expecting me and offered to cooperate. We walked into the chapel where the closed casket was placed, and talked about where he would stand and where I might place the microphones. He even helped me move the casket so I could arrange my equipment.

"About how long will the service be?" I asked.

"About thirty minutes," he said. I explained that I could only record fifteen minutes on one side of the disk, and would miss a few seconds of his service while I turned the disk.

"That's no problem," said the minister. "Just give me the high sign when you're ready to turn it over." I had no idea what he had in mind.

"Will there be any songs during the service?" I asked, thinking further about mike placement.

"Songs?" he asked. "How many would you like?" Whoa, I thought. Suddenly I understood that this funeral, oddly enough, was yet another form of show business. In the case of the funeral, the music, the staging, the costumes, and many of the rituals were designed to offer comfort to the friends and relatives of the deceased. After that I relaxed, convinced that show biz is show biz, whether on a stage, at the movies, in Congress, a church, or a funeral parlor.

When the service was about to begin, I knelt in front of my machine, donned my earphones, and began recording. When the end of the first side approached fifteen minutes later, I discreetly held up a hand as a signal.

The minister, preaching enthusiastically, saw my signal from a corner of his eye and stopped in mid-sentence. Bowing his head, he said, "Let us pray." After I turned the disk and signaled again, he said, "Amen," and continued the sermon, never missing a beat. When the service was over, he wouldn't leave to lead the funeral procession until he'd heard the first hymn played back.

But the most bizarre part of the episode was yet to come. That evening, when I delivered the recording to the client, he invited me in to meet the grieving family and sit with them while they listened to the entire funeral service yet again. Which I did.

This experience, along with others in the world of broadcasting, served to stretch my perceptions of how the world worked; they allowed me to peek into corners I never knew existed. But for me, something was lacking. Would I spend the rest of my life recording funerals? After doing it a few times, where was the challenge?

At the end of the semester, and after receiving commercial and amateur radio licenses, I accepted a full-time radio job in Norfolk, Virginia. Now I was getting somewhere. Norfolk was much closer to the big time. The job was more exciting, especially since I worked the early morning shift. Remembering my experiences with farmers who worked in the middle of the night, I began inviting listeners to call and tell me why they weren't in bed.

The response was unexpected and gratifying. The milkman called, the cop on the beat called, taxi drivers called. Talking to folks just coming off their night shifts was fun and educational. They seemed thrilled that somebody noticed.

The pay was good, and Jeanne added to the family moneypot through her job at Orkin. She also added excitement whenever she brought home another exotic dead bug for us to admire.

Life rollicked along until one day I found myself fantasizing about becoming really successful and moving up to big time radio/TV work. But in the middle of that perfectly grand fantasy—wham!—I realized that kind of success would buy me the dubious privilege of living in New York, Chicago, or Los Angeles. (You know the old joke: First prize is a week in Philadelphia—second prize is *two* weeks in Philadelphia.) After living in dreary Greenwich Village flats, I just couldn't see happiness unfolding in those large metropolises. Short-sighted, perhaps, but my radio aspirations dissolved, and, after serious discussion with my wife, we decided to return to Ohio University to tilt at a master's degree in experimental psychology.

six

More Schooling

FTER EARNING THE DEGREE A YEAR LATER, I was asked to join the psychology faculty for a year before trudging toward a doctorate elsewhere. So I taught Introductory Psychology and Advertising Psychology. Like other faculty, I never had any training in teaching university students, so I just did to them what had been done to me. We weren't accountable for our results, after all, so it didn't seem to matter if our teaching techniques were inefficient or self-centered. I'd never taken the advertising psych course as an undergraduate, so that was another example of the blind leading the blind. Even so, the experience nudged me closer to the world of human behavior.

Called one day for a meeting with the department head, I found myself being asked to take over an Educational Psychology course. The regular professor had died or something and a replacement was needed—now.

"But I've never taken Educational Psychology," I protested. "I wouldn't have anything to teach."

"Doesn't matter. You'll have the rest of the week to prepare. Here's the textbook and the exams," he said, handing me a book and a sheaf of multiple-choice tests.

Needless to say, I did a terrible job. My audience consisted of experienced classroom teachers—fine educational combat troops—and I had nothing to teach them they didn't already know. It was an embarrassing episode, and, I thought, a gross disservice to the students. Those teachers were kind, however, and didn't harass me about my ignorance.

Later, I learned my ignorance was less important than my presence—just being there helped those poor captive souls earn another piece of the academic holy grail—credit hours. (Actually learning anything seemed, at best, secondary.) Once again, things weren't what they seemed.

That wasn't the only eye-opener. During a faculty meeting, the department chairman announced that we had a little money in the slush fund and asked for suggestions for its possible deployment. I naively suggested we buy a recorder and record some of our lectures. By listening to ourselves, I offered, we might improve our teaching. The room exploded with silence. The motion passed—who could vote against improving instruction? But as you might guess, the issue died from neglect. I remember having to think about that one awhile before I understood its significance—what you don't know about your own performance won't hurt you. In other words, don't rock the status quo.

On several occasions I asked our dean—a history professor—to attend at least one of my classes so he could better evaluate my work. His response? "If I didn't think you were a good teacher, we wouldn't have hired you." Uh-huh. End of evaluation.

I began to realize that "education" was more about teaching (i.e., going through the instructing motions), and much less about learning.

Calculus? You're kidding, right?

With the exception of the above, the pinball flippers minded their own business until I entered graduate school at The State University of Iowa in 1951 in the quest for a doctorate. I soon discovered the experimental psychology curriculum was heavily loaded with math and statistics courses. I wondered what had happened to the psychology I signed up for.

I was even required to sign up for a course in calculus, for God's sake! Taught by an ex-Iowa farmer. Good grief! In spite of my preconceptions, though, this was the best-taught course of my entire three years. Each day the instructor picked one student to answer a string of questions—not as a test, but as small steps leading the student to the derivation of the theorem for the day. From that day forward that theorem was referred to by that student's name. "As you see, Thinwhistle's theorem applies here," the instructor would announce. At no time did any of the students feel insulted or demeaned. I think the positive attention encouraged them to work even harder.

It finally occurred to me: even though only one student was picked to answer questions, we were all active participants. Like sports fans rooting for the home team, or an audience at a quiz show, we all answered the questions in our own minds. As a result, we were actively engaged in the learning at all times. Though "mathematically challenged," to use a smarmy PC term, I came to experience the beauty of mathematics. That ex-farmer was an education all by himself. Imagine! Learning could not only be engaging and exciting, it could be exciting in the subjects students usually dreaded.

The summation operator caper

Though math was relevant to the equation-drenched curriculum, the ability of the faculty to communicate that content was sometimes less than sterling. One of my enthusiastic statistics professors wrote equations on the blackboard with his right hand while erasing with his left, and at the same time complained about the lack of adequate writing space. Though erasing gave him enough room to begin a new string of equations, it didn't give us enough time to take notes and focus on the concepts simultaneously.

One particularly vexing topic was that of the summation operator, a commonly-used mathematical symbol rich with meaning. I left the lecture on this symbol completely dazed. I vowed somehow to understand the concept. To do so, I button-holed several sources for information, after which I wrote a step-by-step explanation for myself, including examples. When I finished with the final rewrite, I finally felt I understood the fundamentals.

Then something unexpected happened. Word had spread about my project when I asked for help in understanding the concept, and other graduate students began asking for a copy. Soon after, the faculty asked for copies. I was flattered, of course, but back then copies weren't easy to make! (They practically had to be chiseled into stone tablets). Fortunately, the department offered to make copies on their Hectograph machine (a prehistoric copying process involving gelatin and purple ink).

This, and similar experiences, taught me a lesson repeated many times since. Students are usually hungry for enlightenment and understanding. Unless they're enrolled strictly for the credit, they truly want to learn what is being taught. But often careless teaching denies them that enlightenment. Haphazard instruction—as happens when explanations are offered with undefined terminology, incorrect assumptions are made about students' current knowledge, students are required to focus on the subject while simultaneously taking notes, little or no opportunity is provided for periodic practice, and feedback is delayed or non-existent—creates monumental obstacles to learning.

Those are only some of the obstacles strewn in the path of the learner. In other words, a student's willingness to learn is often impeded by instructors unschooled in the art of teaching (university faculty, for example, are seldom required to demonstrate teaching skill before, or after, being hired), by poorly designed environments, and by carelessly compiled materials. Little wonder my fellow grad students grasped at my little summation operator instruction, which was only meant to help me understand the concept.

Though I had seen how writing step-by-step explanations of difficult concepts could aid in my own personal understanding, I still had no conscious interest in devoting myself to the intricacies of effective instruction. My goal at that time was to become a research psychologist and shuffle about in a white lab coat looking for Universal Truths. Even so, my growing habit of breaking ideas into their component parts proved a great aid in communicating intricate concepts.

By the way, that little paper on the summation operator was printed by the psychology department and distributed to graduate students and faculty for several years after my departure—after careful removal of my name as author!

Writing is hard work

Writing papers to aid my own understanding was one thing—writing to satisfy a dissertation professor—and committee—was another. I couldn't write my way across a mud puddle—my undergraduate English teacher had told me so. "Don't ever think of yourself as a writer," she'd said. Unfortunately, I believed her and the self-assessment stuck with me for decades. Believe it or not, I still don't think of myself as a writer. When someone asks me what I do for a living, it never occurs to me to reply, "I'm a writer."

Nonetheless, the rules said a dissertation had to be produced. Words came hard, coherent sentences even harder. For some reason the sentences were expected not only to make sense, but to follow one another and relate to the subject at hand. That was so hard, the tiny act of changing paper in the typewriter was enough to knock a gestating thought all the way to Hoboken.

Desperate to succeed, I purloined some fan-fold paper from the teletype machine at the local radio station and typed my draft thereon. Now I could type forever without having to change the paper. When it came time to submit a few pages to my dissertation professor, I simply tore off what I'd written and handed him the next segment of what became known as the "Dread Mager Scrolls." His good nature saved the day and eventually the drafts improved (as I'm sure he knew they would).

During those excruciating days I was asked to submit a paper for publication in the Institute of Electrical and Electronic Engineers (IEEE) Student Quarterly. After suitable protestations, I wrote, and submitted. When the article, *Are Automated Universities Passé?* was published several months later, I was astonished at how my writing had improved. I read it through a time or two and thought it sailed along pretty well.

Then, a month or so later, my edited manuscript was returned, and I couldn't believe the number of red marks defacing my pristine pages. The published article said what I'd intended for it to say, but the editor (bless her soul) had made dozens of modifications. On careful study I had to conclude that each was warranted. So much for my "much improved" writing. The episode whacked me with a new appreciation for the skill and, I'm convinced, indispensability, of a good editor (*finding* one is another matter). Ever since, I've tried to avoid publishing anything of significance unless it is first touched (gouged?) by the magic wand of an editor.

Oh, rats

During the struggle with statistics, calculus, and the French version of *Les Trois Mousketaires*, I was blessed with an opportunity to learn about the love life of the white rat. (These creatures and I weren't strangers—I usually had a white rat or two under my bed during my younger years. My cousin, a nurse, arranged permission for me to hang around the lab at the hospital where she worked. There was usually a spare rat I could take home as a pet.)

During graduate school, I spent one year in charge of the lab rat breeding program. So I became the "Madam" of the rat world and wielded the final decision about who slept with whom . . . and for how long. That gave me a feeling of power. But before your imagination loses its grip, you should know it wasn't all sex, sex, sex in the rat world. As I had so often discovered when peeking behind the scenes of the people world, there was a very different underside. On occasion, rat mamas ate their young.

Though I'd had no training in rat psychotherapy, it was my job to intervene, so I'd remove the surviving babies from cannibal-mama's cage and try to find another home for the tiny orphans. To accomplish this humanitarian task, I'd try cajoling another mother into adopting the little tykes and treating them as her own. Finesse and a smooth line of sweet-talk were the order of the day. Sometimes it worked, sometimes not—even though I offered my sexiest smile and tastiest Purina Rat Chow as inducements. (I still wish I had a recording of myself trying to cajole these females into adopting six or eight orphans.) One day one of my mamas gave birth to a living litter of *eighteen*. I was so proud I handed out cigars.

Why rats? Were we pretending rats were like humans—that conclusions drawn from rat research could be extrapolated to human beings? Nothing so arrogant. In fact, just the opposite. Our goal was to conduct research designed to verify or refute a learning theory, not to discover principles of immediate practical value. For that purpose, white rats served quite well. Cute, too.

The conviction was that once we understood what made the white rat tick, we could work our way up the food chain to the human being. That approach probably wouldn't have taken more than a hundred years or so of staring at rats sniffling their way along the byways of a maze. The research process is a necessary activity, but not the most captivating.

To over-simplify, the approach we followed was to set up conditions and see what happened. Something like poking a guy's behind with a cattle prod and measuring how high he jumps. We could then vary the conditions and try the experiment again. Is the height of his jump influenced by the voltage of the prod? Time of day? Amount of caffeine in his system? Thickness of his skin? You see the possibilities.

But, as I would soon discover, there was another way to go about it.

Skinner who?

During Iowa days, Albert Bandura and I occupied offices across the hall from one another. He was a year ahead of me in his doctoral quest, and beyond brilliant. No matter the hour, it was unusual not to find him at his desk working. Though he didn't welcome interruptions, he took time to answer the occasional question I carried across the hall.

One day I noticed him reading a book written by a Dr. B. Frederick Skinner and asked him about it. I knew Skinner's name was mentioned only in hushed terms around the department and was surprised that Bandura appeared to be openly studying his works. Dr. Kenneth Spence, head of the psychology department, was a serious proponent of the Clark Hull approach to learning theory, and didn't take kindly to comments lauding the work of Skinner. When Bandura agreed to lend me the Skinner book, I wondered if I shouldn't sneak it across the hall in a brown paper bag.

Reading that book was like shining a light into a dark room. Skinner's approach was quite different from the one we followed. Rather than set up conditions and conduct an experiment to find out what happened, he *first* decided on the desired result and then tried to discover how to make that result happen. Thus, instead of skewering with the cattle prod and measuring how high the hapless "prodee" jumped, Skinner first decided how high a jump he wanted. Only then did he set out to discover what it took to reach that goal.

This represented a monumental difference in orientation: (a) do something, then measure the results to find out what happened, or (b) decide on a desired result, and organize your efforts to achieve it.

While we purposely studied a sophisticated theoretical structure with little discernible practical value, Skinner and colleagues actually applied their approach to the real world of behavior. While we bent our brains conducting experiments aimed at verifying a theory (a legitimate and valuable enterprise, by the way), Skinner taught pigeons to work as quality control inspectors on pharmaceutical production lines—tirelessly picking the bad pills from the moving conveyor belt—without ever going on strike for more birdseed. During WWII he also designed a bombsight several times more accurate than anything the military had (a pigeon steered the warhead by pecking at a visual image of the target). Wow! Reading Skinner's work and hearing about it from those studying with him was a serious whack, but it would be some time before an opportunity arose to put those insights to use.

seven

Learning about Learning

ON THE DAY THE DOCTORATE WAS CLUTCHED SAFELY IN MY HANDS, I stared at it and wondered what I could do now that I couldn't do the day before. After three years of hard work, the degree itself seemed anti-climactic. Mentally taking stock, I ticked off the skills I thought I'd accumulated: I was damned good at breeding rats, I could fabricate equipment for other students to use in their research, I had a grasp of learning theory and statistics, and I understood the components of a well-designed experiment. I could also make a manual Monroe calculating machine sing.

But something was missing. Aha! There it was! Though the research structure was in place, I hadn't actually changed anybody's behavior. Other than my summation operator paper, I hadn't applied a learning theory to teach anybody anything. Except, of course, teaching white rats to run a maze. ("All right now, class. Keep your tails to yourself and pay close attention while I demonstrate . . . ")

Wham! The significance of Dr. Skinner's work again whacked

me about the head and shoulders. What good was all that theory unless it could be applied?

Fortunately, I would soon face an opportunity to change as many pounds of behavior as my skill and skull could manage. I signed on for a job at a civilian research unit attached to Fort Bliss, Texas—the Human Resources Research Office (HumRRO). There, research focused on discovering improved training methods for the installation and maintenance of complex electronic systems. Could this be what I wanted to do when I grew up? It sounded promising, but I still wasn't sure. I would soon find out. With a fresh degree in hand and a newly-minted son in a basket, we packed our sparse belongings and moved south. The new assignment provided a welcome change in climate; after shoveling through three snow-filled winters in Iowa City, the El Paso desert couldn't have been more inviting.

The other arrows in my quiver were paying off, in the form of a higher salary offer than expected. The electronics training, along with my military experience, were now good as gold, as were my FCC Commercial Radio License and fabricating experience. Extra-curricular activities count. Once again I mentally thanked the anonymous person who had advised me to do *something*.

Maximum exhilaration

If the ideas described in Dr. Skinner's book had been exciting, the next explosion of light was energizing.

Sometime during 1958, Norman Crowder visited our research unit at HumRRO and showed us an invention called a "scrambled book." (You're unlikely to have heard of him, probably because he wasn't an academician driven by the need to publish.) Programmed instruction was the hot issue of the time—the keystone of a revolution in education, according to some. (Nutty aside: The really hot debate of the day had to do with whether programming was spelled with one "m" or two. Nothing like focusing on the really important things.)

Programmed instruction was a way of presenting content in steps small enough to be grasped by the intended audience. Each small step was followed immediately by confirming feedback. The procedure was simple: A student was presented with a small amount of information and asked a question to test understanding. The student's response (writing a response, pushing a button, speaking a word or phrase) was followed immediately by information confirming or correcting the response.

At the time, the approach most in vogue was the linear program, in which students responded to a fixed linear sequence of questions called "frames." This approach, developed by Dr. Skinner, offered the same instruction in the same sequence to everyone, regardless of background or experience.

You can imagine our excitement when we learned that Crowder's "scrambled book" approach, as opposed to the linear approach, was *interactive*; it could be designed to adjust to each student's prior knowledge. The learners' responses determined what part of the program they went to next. That way, students were required to study only what they didn't yet know—at least, according to the theory. In effect, a student received no instruction at all until his/her responses were incorrect. It was an efficient way to organize the instruction.

A few of us immediately began experimenting with the technique, and developed several small pieces of programmed instruction in both the branching (interactive) and linear formats. For example, one member of our research team knew from experience that the most difficult concept for freshman chemistry students was that of "molar solutions." He set out to create a branching program on that subject. When he tested the result on his students, they reported that the concept of molar solutions was now easy to understand.

Branching programmed instruction was our introduction to a form of instruction that took the nature and needs of the individual student into account. Teaching was no longer all about the teacher and the acts of instruction—it was about the student and about achieving valued results. Both we, and our tryout students, were delighted. Now we had a way to design instruction systematically. It was a heady feeling. Thanks to this, and the insights gained from Skinner's work,

I was developing a more serious commitment to the improvement of instruction. The concepts on which programmed instruction were based provided a much more systematic framework within which to work than the loosey-goosey "winging it" approach. As a result, it seemed we could discover and apply more meaningful ways to improve learning.

Radar VI

Other important insights were there for the taking at HumRRO.

At that time, the Army operated a 32-week training course for radar technicians. On graduation, the technicians were assigned to a radar installation serving as part of our Air Defense System. But there were problems. The field performance of the newly-graduated technicians was poor, and it took a long time for them to improve—they didn't become truly proficient until they had had two years of experience on the job *after* completing the 32-week course. In other words, they had to learn on the job much of what they should have learned in training.

With military concurrence, the Research Unit established a project to develop an improved course. The team consisted of Lloyd Hitchcock, James E. Whipple, and me. As one of the principal investigators, my first assignment was to divine the objectives of the Army course. At the time, objectives were "understood," but not written down. We needed them written down, however, as they would be the targets against which we would evaluate our experimental course. We needed them written down so we could compare student performance produced by each course against the same standard. To do that, we had to answer the question: "What are trainees expected to be able to do when ejected from the school into the real world?" Caricaturing the conversation with the school commandant:

Me: May I please have a list of the course objectives?

C: What's an objective?

Me: Darned if I know. I'll go back to my office and figure it out.

At that time, there were things *called* objectives in the educational literature, but I could find none that said anything about intended outcomes in anything but abstract terms (e.g., know, understand, appreciate, etc.). Bloom's *Taxonomy of Educational Objectives* had been published in 1956, for example, but the statements included in that book were too general to be of help. At best, they were broad descriptions of goals; they weren't objectives describing useful outcomes. This was hardly a surprise; the *Taxonomy* was intended to help teachers communicate with one another more effectively, not to offer a precise way of describing instructional outcomes.

In due course, our draft objectives (derived from our meager knowledge of the hardware and best guesses) were offered to the Colonel and his staff. After some reviewing and pecking, we arrived at a final version. We then used that signed document—the course objectives—both to identify relevant and irrelevant content and practices in the existing curriculum, and to select content and practices for our experimental course.

Here's some of what we found when analyzing the existing course. The first week consisted of mathematics. Why should technicians have to spend a week learning math? To help them through the following twelve weeks of Basic Electronics, we were told. And why should they need twelve weeks of Basic Electronics theory just to install and maintain a radar system? They didn't, but it was always done that way. Why should they be instructed in the art of soldering when policy forbids using soldering irons in the field? Well . . . techies should know how to solder.

Keeping the primary purpose in mind—graduating maintenance technicians who could actually *repair* the system in the field—we drafted the course. First, we replaced the week of math with four days of operator training (how to "drive" the system) and a day of troubleshooting (locating and clearing malfunctions) practice. This new curriculum was revealing to trainees in at least two ways. First, many had never seen a completely functional system before; it was a revelation to some that the system could actually track a target and lock a weapon onto its radar return signal. Second, at the end of that first week they knew they could already solve approximately a third of the troubles they would encounter in the field. They knew because they'd already had practice in solving those problems.

Next, we eliminated about sixty percent of the Basic Electronics course. That was politically risky, as BE was taught by a separate administration, with separate buildings and separate staff. To suggest that much of the BE content was irrelevant to preparing functional maintenance techs was like suggesting that babies might be conceived without sperm. (It is an unexamined truism that electronic equipment cannot be installed and maintained without training in BE theory. It is a false, but nonetheless pervasive, belief.)

The remainder of the course focused on learning to troubleshoot hardware problems, including a good deal of practice on the actual equipment itself. Our final course was only 26 weeks long, not 32. Had we not been certain it would lead to political suicide, it would have been several weeks shorter than that.

After crafting a three-hour performance test, we pilot-tested the course on a group of trainees. At the end of the course, the three-hour performance test was administered to one graduate at a time; trainees were asked to locate and clear real problems in functioning radar systems. No multiple-choice questions. Nothing but real performance on live systems—as prescribed by the objectives.

The results were revealing. There was little similarity in the performance of the two groups. The brand new graduates of our 26-week course performed as well or better than the graduates of the 32-week course who already had 18 months of field experience besides. Because the test required actual performance on real equipment, the results were difficult to dispute.

A number of factors led to these results, and one in particular is worth highlighting. Regardless of the type of equipment, about a third of the malfunctions are caused by the operator. My own experience confirms this to be true almost anywhere in the world, for equipment large or small, military or civilian, business or personal. Operators regularly leave switches and controls in the wrong position, or leave portions of the system unplugged. Then, when they later note something is wrong, they immediately conclude there is a problem with the hardware and call the tech. (And why not? That's what they're usually trained to do.) Techs trained in the traditional way then run directly to their wiring diagrams to hunt for the malfunction, instead of checking for causes induced by careless, distracted, or inadequately trained operators.

Just teaching our trainees to operate the system made them begin to look like wizards when they made a malfunctioning radar system sing merely by closing an interlocked door. It did wonders for their motivation and self-confidence, and convinced me that all instruction should begin by giving students hands-on experience with the target subject.

The experiment taught me something far more important than techniques of instructional design. I learned that bad or careless instruction can destroy motivation, morale, self-efficacy, and self-confidence. For example, trainees who couldn't master the math week were thrown out of the course. Many of these men were not new recruits; they were seasoned soldiers wanting to upgrade themselves into the "modern" Army. When they were discarded after one week merely because they couldn't master the math (*all* of which was irrelevant to radar maintenance), it was more than a slap in the face. It was humiliating and demeaning, and several of these men shed tears when told of their "failure."

This amounted to a callous squandering of motivated human beings, depriving the school of people eager to improve their value to their employer. I don't believe it was done deliberately; it was simply the way things were done at the time. Nonetheless, it was a heart-wrenching example of a waste of human capability that touched me deeply. It would be nice if this were an isolated instance of instructional insensitivity. Unfortunately, such examples were and are found everywhere—they remain the coin of the realm.

Another example of instructional insensitivity might be listed under the heading of Untested Assumptions. The school had imposed another prerequisite for the course, one that prevented enrollment of color-blind personnel. It seemed sensible: after all, wires and components were color-coded, leading some to conclude that technicians should be able to detect color. The problem with that reasoning was revealed when the color-blind students secretly slipped into the course performed as well as those with normal color vision.

It was no mystery. Skilled technicians learned better than to rely on color-coding as a basis for troubleshooting. They had to—the El Paso desert heat quickly melted the wire colors into gray. We couldn't begin to guess how many potentially competent people had been rejected because of this unexamined assumption.

Experiences such as these improved my ability to identify obstacles to learning. Unfortunately, those obstacles, then and now, almost always must be laid at the feet of the faculty, the administration, the physical and emotional environment, or politics. Eliminating them was—and is—often easier said than done.

eight

In Search of Outcomes

THE RADAR VI EXPERIMENT HIGHLIGHTED the enormous gap between what was known—and what was practiced—in the quest for effective instruction. It showed us that students could learn more in less time than previously required. It showed us that when we made the objectives known, irrelevancies and redundancies in existing courses became obvious as if by magic—for example, the week of math in the radar system troubleshooting course. We were reminded that critical, but missing, components were also easy to spot—like the missing operator training.

Similar insights had appeared during our experimentation with programmed instruction. Because the branching format allowed us to teach only what a student didn't yet know, we could eliminate much— sometimes all—of the instruction. A clearly-stated objective focused students' energies, and encouragement to study only what they didn't know made the process more user-friendly. With that simple format we fantasized eliminating at least half the world's instruction. That was an exciting thought. But radical . . . and potentially dangerous. (Think about who has heavy investments in the educational status quo, and about how far they might go to protect it.)

At the time, instructors focused on the *process* of instructing, not on its *outcomes*. Since they were free to select course content on the basis of "I'm the expert and I know what students need to learn," there was often little consistency between two or more courses bearing the same name. Tests asked questions intended to reveal how much students learned of whatever might have been taught, rather than whether objectives had been accomplished. The gap between those two orientations—process-driven and outcome-driven—is so great that to this day many are unable to make the leap from one to the other. Many cannot even see that there *is* a gap.

Jim Whipple, of our El Paso research unit, made the difference clearer with an analogy: Suppose you listed the steps for making a pot of coffee, asked someone to make one, and graded the results. The *process*-oriented instructor might give a 90% grade to a coffee-maker who omitted only the step of inserting the coffee. The *outcome*-oriented instructor would grade the same performance zero because the objective—making coffee—was not accomplished. Shifting one's mindset from process to outcome is difficult at best; for those with huge investments in the process-oriented approach, it is nearly impossible.

Facilitating that shift would have to begin with the objective. With a clear statement of purpose it might be easier to envision the road to its accomplishment; it might also be easier to see what portions of existing instructional content were unrelated to the desired accomplishment. This was not a new idea. Almost everyone uses objectives at one time or another. Business objectives, military objectives—even the grocery list represents an objective of sorts. The only place I knew where outcome-oriented objectives were not used routinely for describing performance targets was education. There, the statements called objectives usually described process rather than expected results.

The more I worked with the concept the more I shook my head when reading fuzzy statements such as these, that alleged to describe intended outcomes:

- To develop a feel for economics;

- To understand the workings of a modern dental office;

- To teach students to express themselves clearly;

- To develop a positive public image;

- Understand the four types of bargaining relationships;

- Internalize a growing awareness of one's self; or to

- Be recreationally literate.

These formulations are of little use to an instructional developer striving to accomplish demonstrable performance results. Useful, perhaps, as vague statements of intent, and more numerous than cockroaches, but they say nothing about expected results—objectives they are not. Worse, most focus on the instructional process itself. I had to devise something better.

In my spare time, I tried a number of formulations, completely focused on how to state desired outcomes in a way that would help students to achieve them.

One day I asked myself, "Why not write a branching program on how to write objectives?" That would serve two purposes: Provide further practice with the programming concept, and at the same time force me to clarify my thinking. I began, slowly, doing exactly that. But the objectives project wouldn't be completed for some time.

What do they know?

Meanwhile, we whacked away at our research projects at HumRRO. Though we did our best to advance the state of the art through our literature searches and experimentation, I wondered whether some people in industry might know something we didn't know about the art and science of learning. What if we weren't as knowledgeable as we thought? What if others were doing it better while we lurched along in ignorance? Would it hurt to ask?

The idea was perceived as radical by some and met with some derision, but in the end my proposal was accepted. I contacted the training directors of half a dozen corporations and asked to visit their training facilities. All agreed, and I prepared a questionnaire to guide my observations.

I inspected training facilities, pawed through materials, and listened carefully to descriptions of their practices. I sat in on classes and interviewed students and instructors. On returning to El Paso, I prepared and submitted my report. One or two observations were useful.

First, the training establishments I visited tended deliberately to blur the distinction between classroom and laboratory, between lecture and hands-on practice. Rather than operating a classroom over here, and a lab over there, they blended them into a single learning environment. Students learned content where they could look at and fondle the objects of their learning. (Obviously, this practice didn't lend itself to all subjects.) This arrangement not only made it easier for the instructor to manage the learning, it increased the amount of practice possible during a given period of time. The arrangement also reduced the amount of lecturing, and, as students were learning to do it the way they would do it on the job, there was no need to invoke the artificial concept called "transfer of training." Because what they practiced during the course and did on the job were one and the same, there was nothing to "transfer."

Secondly, at one company I visited, promotion to instructor was a lateral move. Because no additional money was offered to those "elevated" to instructor, clever management found other ways to make their instructional staff feel special. For example, only instructors were allowed the freedom to dress according to personal preference. That alone made them the envy of their peers. In addition, each was issued a brass-plated chalk holder. It proved an inexpensive, but useful, status symbol. Finally, management engaged the services of a retired fly rod maker and commissioned him to make customized spun glass pointers for each trainer. That was truly special.

While industry didn't appear to have any learning secrets, there was more comprehensive appreciation for blending theory with experience in the environment in which the theory was to be applied. Theory and practice are different animals, despite claims to the contrary. (Knowing the "theory" of tubas does not automatically confer an ability to play one.) That's why products are tested under real world conditions before being marketed. The theory might be sound, but the application might require serious product modification before it could be used at all. For example, the radar system referred to earlier sported a one-hundred-pound power supply module— mounted at eye-level! It worked, but only the strongest could remove it for repairs. It was completely impractical in the user environment.

Industry has a far better grasp of the differences between theory and practice—as well as the necessity of practice under real world conditions—than is often found in academe. In sum, I found the industry-exploration project broadened my knowledge of how others viewed the mission of creating competent graduates. Curiously, my colleagues were convinced my travels were nothing more than a paid job-hunting scam. They were wrong, but the myth persisted for several years.

From government to industry

It was time for a giant whack. While exploring programmed instruction concepts, I responded to a call for papers at the 1960 annual conference of The Institute for Radio Engineers (IRE). I submitted a paper titled "Preliminary Studies in Automated Instruction," describing work we'd been doing with the programming concept.

That started a choo-choo train terminating in Palo Alto.

Dr. Ed Herold, vice president for research at Varian Associates, was an active member of the IRE (later renamed The Institute for

Electrical and Electronic Engineers, or IEEE). As program chairman for the 1960 conference, he decided to offer a panel discussion on the exciting new topic of programmed instruction.

First choice for a spot on the panel was, of course, Dr. Fred Skinner, the famous Harvard professor who had formulated the linear programming method. Dr. Skinner accepted the invitation to participate. At that point, Ed Herold ran out of people who knew much, if anything, about programmed instruction—it was that new. Needing three more speakers to fill out his panel of four, he next invited Dr. Harvey White, a physics professor, and Dr. Ray Carpenter, a professor of education. At least they were active in the ed biz.

That still left one slot open. Desperate by now (he told me later), he resorted to rummaging through the papers submitted for the convention program. He discovered the paper I'd submitted, and called me to determine whether I had horns. Satisfied that I didn't, he invited me to join as the fourth on his panel.

The session went well, and afterward, Dr. Skinner and I went off for a private lunch (it was the first time I'd met him). It ended all too soon, but I remember leaving the table believing him to be one of the kindest, gentlest, most caring human beings I'd ever met—in addition to being dazzlingly bright.

Shortly thereafter, I received an offer to establish a behavioral research lab in an environment populated entirely by physicists and engineers. Varian Associates in Palo Alto was considering entering the education business by way of teaching machines, and a small lab would allow them to sample the waters before taking the plunge.

Unexpected wisdom

I was interested in the Varian offer, but a few days after the initial phone call from Ed Herold, I was invited to visit a large electronic firm in New Jersey to interview for the position of Assistant Director of their Technical Institute. That was a little scary, as I'd never held a corporate managerial position.

On the way to the interview, I stopped to visit a good friend and former colleague at Ohio University, Dr. Jesse Day. As it happened, he had another visitor, a manager of the chemistry laboratory for a large Midwest corporation.

Then something special happened. While chatting over a drink, this man proceeded to instruct me in precisely how, and how not, to behave during the upcoming interview. In twenty minutes, he offered me the job interview education of a lifetime. As a result, I approached the interview with more confidence than I had thought possible, and followed my unexpected mentor's advice to the letter. What advice? Two examples. "When asked your ambitions, always talk about the position just above the one for which you are interviewing. That will establish that you're thinking bigger than the offered job and that your ambition is confined to the corporation at hand."

More advice. "You will be taken to lunch and asked if you would like a drink. Order one, but refuse all offers of refills. That will establish you as a safe social drinker. Three or four strangers will appear and join you at the lunch table. These will be managers from other departments. They will be there to look you over and engage you in conversation intended to help them decide how well you might fit into their culture. They'll be testing your social skills."

With advice like that I couldn't lose. The scenario unfolded exactly as predicted, and I returned home feeling good about how I'd handled myself during the entire visit—including "the lunch."

A similar scenario had unfolded during the interview trip to Varian—I got to follow the advice twice in one month. I received a written offer from Varian Associates very shortly thereafter, and heard nothing whatever from the other company. Even so, a decision had to be made. Accept the Varian offer, or wait a little longer in expectation of a response from the East Coast? A few days later I'd still heard nothing . . . not even a phone call. That convinced me I'd somehow blown the interview, and promptly sent an acceptance letter to Varian. The die was cast.

Two months later, I received an offer from the other company, strengthening my conviction I'd made the right decision. A research lab was an environment in which I might pursue the quest for knowledge leading to more elegant learning. Besides, I wasn't interested in working for a corporation that functioned like a bureaucracy and took two months to make up their minds about a job offer.

nine

Sci-fi Land

THE CHANGE IN SCENERY, intellectual and otherwise, could hardly have been more pronounced. I had moved from a government job to industry—from the Texas desert to the heart of what would become Silicon Valley—from an environment populated by psychologists to one occupied by physicists and engineers. It was a different world, and an exciting research environment. Suddenly, I was surrounded by science fiction, as well as people curious about why I was there. Frankly, I felt like a yokel from a sleepy village visiting Broadway for the first time.

After spending a week drafting the outline for a research program, I submitted it to Dr. Herold, director of the research division. He returned it a few days later—with typos circled in red pencil. I'm still embarrassed about that carelessness—it was like standing in front of the King with ketchup stains on my shirt. I had learned lesson number one in the corporate world: To be treated like a professional, act like one. Avoid putting obstacles in the way of the reader or listener.

(Later, when I moved to Paris to work, some kind soul took me aside and advised, "Monsieur, in France, bow-ties are worn by door-to-door salesmen, jockeys, and bartenders." Got it.)

An unexpected visit

While I dug into research at Varian, activity in the programmed instruction arena was heating up. I had barely gotten settled at Varian when I was asked to present at a local programmed instruction conference in San Francisco. I did, and met several more movers and shakers in the new field. Among them was Dr. David Cram, an associate of Dr. Richard Lewis, professor of communication at San José State. (Over the years David has become an indispensable colleague, in part because of his uncanny ability to review an early manuscript draft without pointing out every typo or telling me all the reasons why the idea won't work. Even better, he can do it without destroying my motivation to continue.)

Though I plunged into Varian's research program, I still couldn't resist poking at the branching program on objectives I had started drafting back at HumRRO. I'd already collected a number of examples and tested the characteristics I thought necessary to include. During spare moments (mostly evenings), I honed the draft.

In 1961, I had a visit from Dr. Richard Lewis, who brought with him a man wearing a black bowler hat. The hatted visitor turned out to be John Warriner, editor of Fearon Publishers, San Francisco. Lewis had told him about the "book" I was writing—he'd learned about it from David Cram—and convinced him he ought to look at it. At the time, I didn't refer to my project as a book—it was a collection of typed pages in a loose-leaf binder—and hadn't thought about it being a publishable item.

Lewis raved about the concept while Warriner slowly turned the pages as though they were coated with skunk oil. And rightly so, from his point of view as a publisher of "normal" books. The substance of *this* "book" appeared on the right-hand pages only, with an occasional message—in italics and centered—on a left-hand page.

Rather than reading straight through, the reader was expected to read a page, answer a question and then turn to the page number shown beside the answer selected. The reader would thus move forward, and sometimes back, depending on his/her responses to the material just presented. What respectable publisher would want anything to do with something like *that*?

In spite of Warriner's misgivings, Dick Lewis convinced Fearon Publishers to publish the item. Much later, I learned they did it mainly as a favor to Dick, and also to retain him as one of their authors.

But it's not done that way

The publishing process of the book was a bit of an adventure. When Fearon sent the edited manuscript of the objectives book to the printer, however, they apparently looked at the manuscript and said, "We don't print books this way."

Rather than heed the publisher's instructions, they had set the type in the usual way, starting at the top of the left-hand page—filling the page and then starting at the top of the right-hand page. All the galleys had to be trashed, and they had to reset (re-"lay-out") the entire project. The revised version, too, had to be discarded, because although they managed to get the right-hand pages correct this time, the material on the left was still set wrong—no italics. Third time around was the charm, and printing proceeded.

The original edition was published in 1962 under the title "Preparing Objectives for Programmed Instruction." An awkward title, I admit, but I didn't want to imply that the book was in any way directed toward educators. (The title was later changed to "Preparing Instructional Objectives" when educators began buying the book.)

But wait. Dick Lewis hadn't been the only source of publication impetus. Another strange event had pushed me to complete the project. A year before his and Warriner's visit, and shortly after I established the lab at Varian, Prof. Sid Eboch of San Jose State had asked me to help design a one-day session on programmed instruction for school administrators.

To provide attendees with practice in discriminating stronger and weaker features of both the linear and branching programming formats, we agreed that Sid would write a short linear program with deliberate errors in it, and I would do the same with a branching program.

But what to write about? Finally, I hit on the idea of writing a short branching program dogmatically called, "How to Write Objectives." After all, I already had a draft in hand. With *that* topic, I was certain I could so incense an audience of educators about objectives they'd have trouble discriminating the programming features from the subject matter. A bit mischievous, perhaps, but the object *was*, after all, to offer practice in recognizing useful and useless programming characteristics.

So I branched readers to pages that didn't exist, berated and insulted them when they turned to wrong-answer pages, and sprinkled other poor programming features among the good ones. The resulting program would make great practice grist. It did, and the seminar was hailed a success.

A short time later, however, I learned that two professors at local colleges were using this error-laden program as a *text*—as a *good example*—in their education courses! Of course, I had to put a stop to that, and accelerated my efforts to get the "legitimate" version completed and tested. A short time later, Dr. Lewis appeared, and the rest is history.

After publication I learned how the publisher pondered the economics of the project. It went something like this: "Hmm. Let's see. If we print five thousand copies, give away half that number as promo copies and sell the rest, we'll come out even. Okay, we'll do it." Which they did . . . over and over again. As the impact of the book spread, it was reprinted in batches of fifty thousand, rather than five. It is still in print and has to date been translated into sixteen languages.

Note: I didn't write the objectives book first because I thought the objective was the most important component of an instructional system (there was no "system" at that time), or because I thought it was the first step in the instructional design process. I wrote it first because I perceived a particular need and tried to fill it (and because somebody was using the error-laden draft as a textbook). I was fully aware the book didn't address the important topic of where objectives come from and how to derive them from a real world need. The focus was on trying to develop a useful way of describing important outcomes . . . period. The rest would come later.

Consequences

Though I received many letters commenting favorably on the objectives book, not everyone was pleased. While the concept was considered worthy by many, it was not understood as well as I'd hoped—and still isn't. Though I deliberately aimed the book at the programmed instruction crowd (not educators), the notion of specifying objectives for classroom instruction was beguiling enough that a well-intentioned California legislator managed to pass a law requiring every California teacher to get "Magerized."

Teachers were outraged that anyone should actually pass a law requiring them to describe in advance the instructional accomplishments they were setting out to achieve. Also, The National Council of Teachers of English passed a policy statement against objectives—the very idea of having to say anything specific about their intended instructional results was not to be tolerated. Besides, how could anyone say what students should be able to do as a result of poetry instruction? Or Shakespeare? There followed a heated exchange of letters between supporters and detractors.

In addition to those closing their minds to even trying to making their instructional intentions clear, there was another problem. I had described what I thought to be the useful components of an objective, but had not spelled out the real-world sources from which objectives might be derived. Nor had I described methods for accomplishing such derivations. Though that was not my goal at the time, it bothered some not to be presented with a comprehensive blueprint. This led to thousands and thousands of pseudo-objectives like,

"The student will pass a multiple choice test on (my subject) with a score of 90% or better," or

"The student will be able to recite (something or other) with 100% accuracy in one minute or less."

These gibberish statements describing what teachers were currently teaching in their classrooms were next to worthless, and everybody knew it. (Alas, they are still doing it.) But a California law (the Stull Bill)—at that time—said objectives were required. As a result, teachers throughout that state came to loathe the whole idea. It would be a miracle if that provision of the bill still existed.

It wasn't until later that the "real world," rather than content, was seen as the fountain from which useful objectives should spring. I use the term "was seen" loosely, for it's still misunderstood by many. And it is still baffling to me how the concept of "Decide where you want to go before you select the means for getting there" can be so difficult for some to understand.

ten

Scratching Another Itch

S HORTLY AFTER PUBLICATION OF THE OBJECTIVES BOOK I returned to a project I had begun early during my tenure at Varian (1960–63). Even more urgent than the need for a useful way to describe instructional objectives was an attack on the myriad ways students were mistreated in the name of learning.

Many of the common instructional practices of the day sabotaged any positive feeling for a subject the students had when entering the instructional environment. No matter where I looked, I saw practices that sent students away disliking the subject, the instructor, or both—practices that served to damage students' self-confidence and self-efficacy. Why should students care about objectives—or content—when surrounded by practices and policies leading to fear, anxiety, aversion, and damaged self-esteem? Why should teachers knock themselves out teaching the wonders of geometry, say, when their students left the classroom saying, "If I never hear of *that* subject again it'll be too soon!"

Perhaps I was overly sensitive to teacher activities leading to avoidance behavior by their students—avoidance of a subject, of a teacher, avoidance of school itself. But perhaps not.

Here's what I'm talking about. Imagine being a third-grade student when the teacher selects students for a singing session. She walks around the class and points to each student in turn while pronouncing, "You can sing, you can sing, *you can't sing*, you can sing, etc." The finger pointed at you is accompanied by "You can't sing." A label slapped on—in public. How would that make you feel? What would you tell yourself about your singing potential? And for how many years would that self-image linger?

Or your test performance is perfect, but points are deducted because the class was "unruly" that morning.

Or you were "caught" counting on your fingers and made to stand before the class to be ridiculed.

Or you've done such a good job on your homework assignment the teacher holds you up as a good example to the class. Your classmates shower you with all the epithets reserved for good students—nerd, brain, teacher's pet, grind, geek, etc.

Or you are left-handed, but forced to sit in a desk chair designed for right-handers.

Or you are expected to pay close attention just after finishing lunch, and the teacher rocks back and forth while speaking in a monotone.

Or while trying to demonstrate your enthusiasm for the subject, you blurt out an answer and are told, "Don't try to get ahead of the class!"

And of course, the practice of grading on a curve is engineered into the system, thereby guaranteeing that only a certain percentage of students will be allowed to think of themselves as successful— regardless of their achieved competence. Wherever the number of permissible "A's" and "B's" is dictated by the demands of The Curve, a grade is tempered by the performance of neighbors chancing to sit in the same classroom. No matter how well students master a subject, their grades reflect their performance in relation to their peers, rather than in relation to desired accomplishments. How could such a practice not serve to strangle student motivation to excel?

The unthinking nourishment of avoidance behavior was (and is), rampant and, I believe, explains much of the so-called "dropout" problem. It also explains why "pushout" is a more accurate description. After all, people learn to avoid the things they're hit with; when they're "hit" with an aversive school environment, it shouldn't be a surprise when students opt out. It's an intelligent, reasonable response.

I don't mean to suggest that parents, peers, and television don't contribute their share of damage to constructive attitudes. They do. Educators, however, are *paid* to serve as sources of positive influence. They, at least, should not be among those anointing their charges with avoidance attitudes. The unintended consequences of practices that create avoidance tendencies are serious. One such consequence is diminished self-efficacy (one's belief in his/her ability to perform a given task). Another is the reduced likelihood that a student will ever again willingly make contact with the source of the pain—the subject matter, the instructor, or the institution.

I began including comments about the problem in seminars and workshops as an aid to formulating my thoughts on the topic. Then, at the third annual convention of the National Society for Programmed Instruction (NSPI—now called ISPI), in May 1965, I delivered an invited address titled, "A Universal Objective." In it, I said:

> "The object of this paper is to discuss the importance of designing learning experiences in such a way that they do not teach students to hate the very things they are learning. It is the object to suggest that each and every instructional sequence or event, each and every lecture, each and every program, should have as its number one object the intent to send the student

away from the learning experience with approach
tendencies toward the subject matter equal to or
greater than those with which he arrived."

The paper was published in the May, 1965 issue of the *NSPI
Journal*, by which time I was well into a draft of a book on the subject.

During its development, I asked an independent third party to
interview individual parents (i.e., ex-students) at random, asking
questions such as, "What was your favorite school subject? Why?"
"What subject did you like least? Why?"

Those questions struck a nerve and triggered a flood of
information. My interviewer reported being moved to tears when
listening to the litany of sadistic acts committed and statements made
in the name of education. "You don't have the brains to be in this
class;" "Nothing you do here will ever get you more than a 'C';" and
to a small boy, "For *that*, you can just go sit with the girls!" These
interviews confirmed the importance of exposing the practices that
turn kids on or off, and offered avenues for lessening the damage
caused by those treating students like . . . well . . . slaves. As time
passed, I continued collecting experiences from friends,
acquaintances, and strangers. The emerging patterns were striking.

Though we're born with latent talents, we're not born with built-
in likes and dislikes for the subjects we're exposed to in school. We're
not even born with a fear of snakes. The question was: How do likes
and dislikes—approach and avoidance patterns—develop? For
example, how often did interviewees report an aversion to algebra or
history because they found it too hard? Because they had no "natural"
aptitude for the subject? Seldom! Most reported that their aversions
developed as a result of how they were treated when in the presence
of the subject. In other words, the aversions were orchestrated by
teachers, parents, and poorly-written textbooks.

For example, it is common practice even now to use subject matter
as a form of punishment. "Okay, just for that you can work ten algebra
problems tonight instead of three." Or, "Because of your unruliness,
you can read three chapters of *Silas Marner* tonight instead of just

one." But people learn to avoid the things they are punished with. When they're bashed with the subjects they're supposed to learn to love, they'll learn instead to avoid them! It's one of the ways students are taught to dislike a subject—and learning. (It's also one of the ways parents teach their children to hate *them*.)

The opposite is also true—students learn to like subjects associated with pleasant or rewarding events. When, for example, material is presented in small enough chunks to be understood and mastered, the reward value of that success tends to pull the student forward to the next chunk. A string of such small accomplishments leads to improved self-efficacy, as a result of which students report a growing attraction to the subject.

Contingency management

During the time I was working on the attitude book, I was fortunate to visit the laboratory of Dr. Lloyd Homme, then at the Behavior Systems Division of Westinghouse Learning Corporation in Albuquerque, New Mexico. Lloyd was a brilliant researcher and a major pinball flipper for me. Among other research, he conducted contingency management studies (based on the work of David Premack) with children from local Indian reservations.

"Contingency management" is a technical way of talking about strengthening habits by making a reward contingent upon desired behavior. Lloyd used to call it Grandma's Law: "First you eat your spinach and *then* you can have dessert." Though simple, the technique works only if the reward *follows* the desired performance, and if the reward (technically the reinforcing event) is considered rewarding *by the student*. "All right, you may have one more cookie, but then you've *got* to do your homework" is a backward example of the application of the principle and doomed to failure.

What was truly wonderful was Lloyd's ability to change the hierarchy of preferences for school subjects by applying contingency management techniques. By using a more-preferred activity— arithmetic, for example—to reward small amounts of work on less-preferred subjects—music, say—he could change the hierarchy of preferences. Music would gradually become a more preferred activity (because it was followed by favored arithmetic activity), which could then be used to reward other less preferred activities. In practice the procedure sounded like this: "If you'll work on these music exercises with me for two minutes, then you can do math problems for three minutes." The magical ingredient is the contingency.

One must also make sure the offered rewards are indeed perceived as favorable events *at this moment* by learners. Very small children will work for the privilege of sharpening a handful of pencils, for example, but older kids will not. Lloyd and his associates solved this problem (assuring that rewards are considered rewarding by the student, regardless of how an instructor feels about them) with an invention called the reinforcement menu. Usually this was a piece of paper depicting stick figures engaged in various activities. The student would complete a small amount of work—a few minutes—and then go (they often ran) to the "reinforcement room" to engage in the activity they picked from the reinforcement menu. Two of the most coveted rewards were the privileges of (a) twirling Lloyd around in his swivel chair, and (b) pushing him across the room in that same chair.

The work at Homme's lab was exciting, and because the book I was drafting was about shaping favorable attitudes toward learning, the visit energized my efforts: the pinball bumper had given me another shove. The book was finally published in 1968 under the title, *Developing Attitude Toward Learning*. The more accurate title would have been *Influencing Attitude Toward Learning*, but title testing revealed that the word "influencing" triggered avoidance behavior in teachers erroneously believing their job was not to *influence* students, but merely to "pull out" of them what was already inside. A bizarre notion, but we changed the title anyhow. The title was changed again for the 1997 edition to *How to Turn Learners On . . . without turning them off*—for which I thank the genius at The Center for Effective Performance who thought of it.

My subsequent workshops on the topic seemed partially successful in sensitizing teachers and trainers to the critical role they play in shaping students' attitudes toward learning. It was always gratifying to see eyes widen with the realization that their every move and word might nudge an attitude toward, or away from, the subject at hand: "My God, I'm going to have to be careful of everything I say and do from now on!" What ever made them think their words and actions didn't have serious consequences in the minds of their students? What made them think, "Don't do as I do—do as I say," was anything but pompous rhetoric?

As many of us have learned, exhortation is probably the least effective way to influence behavior.

eleven

Logical Sequences Aren't

THOUGH CONVINCED I WAS ATTACKING IMPORTANT PROBLEMS with the books I was writing, those had to take a back seat to the Varian research program, where I was officially employed. That research was also interesting and needed to be pushed forward; though eager to write another page or two about attitude, I also could hardly wait to get back to the lab—where a couple of flippers were lying in wait.

One of my projects involved a series of experiments intended to discover what a "logical sequence" of instruction might look like according to the student, rather than to the instructor. Though everyone alleged to instruct in a logical sequence, I noticed that none of the common definitions of "logical" had anything to do with what might be logical from the student's point of view. Content sequences based on historical chronology were called logical: "We'll begin by learning what happened first, then after that . . ." Sequences based on geography were called logical: "First you'll learn what happened

over here, and then we'll follow the map all the way to the sea."
Troubleshooting instruction is often based on the structure of the
target equipment: "We'll start with the antenna, then work our way
to the picture tube." While logical from the point of view of the
wiring diagram, perhaps, I wondered how logical these approaches
were to a learner.

You've no doubt experienced the disjoint between the material
being presented and your own needs. "I don't care about that *now*!"
or, "Don't tell me about the theory until I know what I can *do* with
it," or, "You haven't told me why I should bother to learn this."
Frustrations like these illustrate the sequencing issue. I was convinced
that instructional efficiency might be improved by reducing the
disjoints between instructor and student perceptions of "logical."

To explore the question I first needed a way to visualize what
student-generated sequences of instruction might look like. This
wasn't easy, as it required finding a way into the student's head.
Drilling into the skull seemed impractical (as well as illegal); I needed
to find a less invasive method. After considerable thought and a false
start or two, I created a laboratory technique called "learner-
controlled instruction." This technique, intended only for
experimental purposes, consisted of my pretending to be an "infinite
bag of knowledge" on the subject to be taught—for this experiment,
electronics.

The process is easy to describe, but extremely difficult to execute.
I would invite the student to ask anything she wanted about the
subject, then try to respond in the clearest terms I could muster.
When satisfied with the answer, she would comment or ask another
question. The track of her thinking pattern was recorded for later
review.

This was hard work! It was difficult to respond to a student's
sequence of questions, partly because the questions bounced from
one end of the topic to the other, and partly because I was unprepared
for the experience to seem so unstructured to me. Remember, the
mission was to discover how the *students'* minds thought about the

subject, and somehow to make that track visible and record it.

I found myself thinking, "My God! If I'm finding it so difficult to follow a student when I *know* something about the subject, what in the world must instructors be doing to students when they impose *their* "logical sequence" on students who *don't* know the subject?" It was a humbling revelation.

When I became more skillful at answering students' questions simply, and at a level making sense to them, the students became so strongly motivated they wanted to prolong the sessions. One participant became so excited at what she'd learned during a session, she arrived the following day with a broken radio under her arm. "Today we're going to fix this radio!" she announced. That scared the heck out of me, as the announcement was totally unexpected. But she fixed it. With only a prod or two, she hypothesized that perhaps the batteries were dead. I asked what she thought she ought to do about it. "Change the batteries?" she asked, tentatively. I told her to go ahead. When I tried to point to the battery compartment she snatched the radio off the table and said, "No. I'll do it." You wouldn't believe the elation she expressed when the radio began to work. She could hardly wait to show her physicist husband what she'd accomplished.

That's when I learned—again—that motivating students is a non-problem, and that the use of motivating gimmicks in the classroom is little more than fancy footwork or window-dressing to compensate for poorly-designed instruction.

The next discovery: regardless of protestations to the contrary, everyone knew more about the subject than they were aware of or would admit. "I don't know anything about electronics," was simply not true. Some of what they "knew" was untrue, but incorrect information is information too. I've since found that people always know *something* about the subject being taught—and they ought to be given credit for that knowledge. It strengthens motivation. More than that, it is satisfying and comforting to enter a classroom and be told you won't have to spend time re-learning what you already know.

Most important, perhaps, was discovering that the meaning students assigned to the concept of "simple to the complex" was opposite to the one assigned by instructors. When instructors alleged they taught from "the simple to the complex," they usually meant they taught about the concepts with the fewest variables or building blocks first, then moved toward ever greater levels of complexity. In electronics, for example, it meant beginning with electric charge, magnetism, and individual components first, then moving on to simple circuits, more complex circuits, and so on. Students, on the other hand, reported that the opposite approach—big picture first, moving progressively toward finer levels of detail as instruction continued—made more sense. And why not? It provided referents (conceptual anchors) to which to tie new information. Effective instructors taught that way intuitively—other instructors could be taught to do so too.

The purpose of these experiments had nothing to do with how course content should be derived or who should derive it. It wasn't about giving students freedom to derive their own objectives. The purpose was to record the sequence of connections students made when presented with answers to their own questions, with a view toward later improving content-sequencing procedures.

These experimental encounters radically affected how I viewed the usual instructional practice. Invariably, that process seemed instructor-oriented, often to the point where students' needs were largely ignored. After deciding on the content to be taught, an instructor organized it according to his/her perception of "logical sequence" and then presented it at his/her pace. Ever since, I've tried to give students as much control over their learning—including sequencing—as objectives and circumstances would allow.

As mentioned earlier, motivation never should have been an issue. We've never needed any of the contrived devices so often used to prime the motivational pump. The secret is much simpler: Show students what they are expected to learn to do, provide them with tools and information sources, provide sources of feedback and indicators of progress (reinforcement and guidance), stand by to provide assistance if asked, and then remove the leash.

More humble pie

While the sequencing experiment was underway, I became involved with a more pressing on-the-job issue, that of developing instruction to help production inspectors improve their accuracy at reading analog meters (meters with pointers on them). The reason? Production inspectors in one department were reading meters with little more than 40 percent accuracy. Their erroneous readings were being used as the basis for designing advanced products—the potential for disastrous consequences was considerable. A small piece of instruction was therefore commissioned to attack the problem.

A common error in meter-reading was to take a reading while holding one's eyes in a position convenient to the reader, rather than perpendicular to the face of the meter. Because the pointer was raised from the surface of the printed scale, erroneous readings resulted (the parallax error).

To provide high-density practice in taking correct readings, I fabricated a number of three-dimensional practice items. I pasted photos of a meter scale on the backs of meter-sized plastic sheets of varying thickness, and scribed a pointer on the front. The thickness of the plastic simulated the space between the pointer and the scale. The trainee was instructed to pick up a sheet (about six inches square), and record the reading shown. For immediate feedback, the correct reading was printed on the back. That way, far more practice per unit time was provided than if actual meters had had to be reset after each reading.

To encourage employees to practice at home, I put the practice items into a plywood box shaped like a cosmetic case and covered it with a vinyl skin. At the time, this was much more appealing to the learners (who were all women) than having the items packaged in a gray metal toolbox.

The resulting program-cum-practice worked quite well. After only two *hours* with the program, the workers could read meters with at least 80 percent accuracy, as measured by an automated test with real meters and real readings. I couldn't wait to begin patting myself on the back for delivering such dramatic results.

But wait, he said, one foot poised over the snake pit. As this project proceeded, I wondered what would happen if I used meter reading as the subject for one of my learner-controlled sequencing experiments. Enlisting the participation of volunteers from my "pool," I showed them—one at a time—the testing machine with the meters on it, and said, "These are the meters we want you to be able to read." That *showed* them the objective of the exercise, providing a visual picture of what they were to learn to do. Then I asked, "What, if anything, would you like to know before taking the performance test?" (i.e., fifty readings on four different meters).

To my surprise, they didn't need two days of classroom instruction, or even two hours of carefully-developed programmed instruction. They reached, or surpassed, the 80 percent accuracy level in an average of only *twenty minutes* of learner-controlled Q&A! The *nerve*!

As an interesting aside, 80 percent was set as the criterion level because it matched the average level attained by physicists and engineers. When digital meters were later introduced, accuracy instantly exceeded 99 percent. In other words, performance often can be instantly improved just by redesigning the task—no instruction required. That's worth remembering.

twelve

From Lab to "Real World"

URING THE LEARNER-SEQUENCING EXPERIMENTS, an
opportunity arose to put into practice some of what we'd
learned. John McCann, Chief Factory Engineer of the
Varian Tube Division, had decided to improve the factory engineer
training program and asked if I would help.

The project focused on improving the six-month training program
for new engineers. The current course consisted of two phases: three
months in the classroom followed by three months of rotating
assignments to each department in the division. Though theoretically
there was time for one-on-one expert coaching, in actual practice,
the coaching either didn't happen at all or happened unreliably. In
other words, just being in the presence of wisdom wasn't enough to
guarantee learning—especially when the trainee was perceived by
the expert as a "free body" to assign to scut-work.

We decided to apply a variation of the learner-controlled approach.
Could we make it work in the real world as well as it did in the

laboratory? As the arrival of a new group of engineers was imminent, we drafted objectives as best we could in the short lead time available. When the new hires arrived, they were given tours of the Tube Division's departments and introduced to the key players available to them as information sources. They were given the rough-hewn objectives and told to take charge of their own instruction. Then McCann and staff stepped back to let it happen.

Result? All trainees accomplished the objectives and were ready for assignment within three months, rather than six. This, we believed, was inevitable. Trainees were no longer required to study what they already knew, didn't have to waste time at non-essential tasks, and were free to consult with appropriate resources as needed. Since they knew what they needed to accomplish, they knew what to ask—and what to practice.

Encouraged, we honed the objectives and ran a second group through the program. This time the results were even better. The original training had taken six months—for everyone, whether they needed it or not. The group given control of their instruction, along with the loosely-stated objectives, were ready for assignment within three months. The group given control *and* more precise objectives were all assigned within six weeks. Training time, in other words, was reduced by an average of 75 percent.

McCann was especially pleased when old-timers began grumbling that the new hires knew more about the manufacturing processes than they did after two years on the job. They asked to be put through the same training.

Motivation was so strong it caused something of a problem. Though it wasn't on their list of objectives, trainees wanted to actually assemble a klystron (a high-frequency vacuum tube). They wanted to know what it felt like to step up to the assembly line and put one together. To allow that to happen, an entire assembly line would have had to be shut down—an expensive and impractical proposition.

Since this wasn't a formal experiment, we had to be careful not to read too much into the results. Even so, we concluded that once trainees became comfortable with the learner-controlled process, they were eager to manage their own learning, they worked hard to accomplish the objectives set out for them, and they were willing to call on others' expertise. It was also apparent that with clear objectives and the motivation to accomplish them, learners found ways to do so even when resources were inadequate.

This project confirmed Professor Ohmer Milton's studies at the University of Tennessee which concluded that students NOT allowed to attend class could learn as much or more than those who attended regularly. Milton's experiments were straightforward. One psychology class worked through his course in the usual manner; another class did the same, but was not allowed to attend the lectures. There was never any difference in test performance between the two groups; those not allowed to attend class (except to take the tests) performed at least as well as those who were. Experiments by other researchers using other subject areas revealed similar results.

Let's keep it that way

The following anecdote underlines the point. Some years ago, the principal of a high school in Euclid, Ohio, had a math teacher who complained that his students couldn't learn mathematics.

"It's a waste of time to try to teach them anything," he groused.

The principal replied, "Okay, tell you what we'll do. You give me the exams and we'll post the exam schedule in the hall. We'll tell the students they don't have to come to class, but must take the tests." The math teacher was delighted.

Three things happened. One, students began asking other math teachers for permission to sit in on their classes. Two, they asked one another for help. Three, those recognizing their problem as one of reading, rather than math, asked English teachers for help.

As a result, all their grades improved.

The math teacher then returned to the principal and offered to take his students back, since it now seemed they might be able to learn a little something after all.

"Oh, no," replied the principal. "We've just proved those students can do better in your absence, so we'll just keep it that way!"

I began seeing obstacles to learning in every classroom I observed: obstacles created by instructors, by textbooks, by administrative policy, and by the environment itself. It was like developing a mild form of X-ray vision. It also required me to curb my tongue (a skill I have never totally mastered) when hearing someone tell me how intellectually deficient or unmotivated his or her students were. I always wondered what that teacher was doing to turn them off.

Risky business

While our research continued, there was unexpected fallout in the "real world" from the programmed instruction ferment. A professor of first-semester algebra at a nearby university applied the programming principles to teach the essence of his course. When he did, he discovered his students learned the content of the course so quickly there was time to move on to advanced concepts. He was pleased with that outcome, but then the professor teaching *second*-semester algebra complained bitterly to the dean that *his* subject-matter was being taught by the *first*-semester professor, and that students therefore already knew most of what he intended to teach when they arrived.

That seemed like a strange reaction from someone whose livelihood supposedly was earned by nurturing student competence. If the object was to make students as competent as possible in algebra (or any other subject), why would anyone complain about receiving competent students? Why wouldn't they rejoice instead? Why wouldn't they jump up and down and say, "Oh boy, now I'll have time to teach those advanced concepts I've been yearning to teach!"

Could it be that maintaining the status quo (or some other hidden agenda) was a higher priority than more efficient and successful instruction? In fact, it can be dangerous to create instruction that succeeds "too well." It can be risky to reveal that you know how to teach twice as much in half the time. The existence of entire instructional "empires" can be threatened when they are revealed to be obsolete, unnecessary, or just expensively inefficient. (Recall the danger lurking when we tried to eliminate the Basic Electronics sub-course during the Radar VI experiment.)

Here's an example. One noted corporation had first-line supervisors attend an eighteen-week course intended to teach the basics of supervision. But all was not well; managers complained that boredom and the long time away from home drove some trainees to alcohol or to drugs during the training. A brief analysis revealed there was nothing in that eighteen week course that couldn't easily be replaced by a well tabbed, three ring binder of job aids. Was the course deleted? No. Why not? The man who developed it had become a vice president because of his efforts. Any volunteers for belling the cat?

Shouldn't the news that this entire course could be disbanded without loss be cause for rejoicing? (Rule #1: Follow the money. Rule #2: Follow the vested interests. Rule #3: Vested interests high in the organization trump efficient operation.)

"Legacy courses" such as this exist everywhere; they're the sacred cows of the instructional world, and woe be to those seeking to trample on their sanctity. It would be less politically dangerous to suggest that colleges could earn more money by replacing the football program with a few dozen slot machines.

A useful deliverable

During lulls in the Varian research program, various team members worked at producing useful products. One such was developed by Peter Pipe and Bob Kantor. It was a branching program called *Personalized Instruction on Klystron Principles,* intended for trainees with at least a bachelor's degree in engineering. It was a serious, well-constructed piece of work directed at Varian engineers needing further instruction on the topic. Copies were distributed throughout the plant and received good reviews from management. The management recognition helped dispel rumors that we were running a bordello for women (only employees' wives were available to participate in our experiments).

The high quality of the work was hardly a surprise. Peter is a remarkable man. An RAF pilot during WWII, he joined us with the practical programming experience gained as senior editor at Western Design (a Santa Barbara corporation). In addition, he is an experienced journalist whose skill with words never ceases to amaze me. My eyes always bulge when I see him replace an entire string of words with only one. That happened with great regularity, and day by day he patiently nudged me in the direction of better writing. He still does. (During his review of this manuscript, Peter reminded me that editors sometimes *add* words as well as delete them. Picky, picky.)

"New Technology" fever

The early sixties roiled with activity in the field of instructional technology, years during which programmed instruction was proclaimed by enthusiasts as the new "sliced bread." It was going to revolutionize education. Uh-huh. Ed Herold put this enthusiasm into perspective. He drew a curve to illustrate his words as he described it.

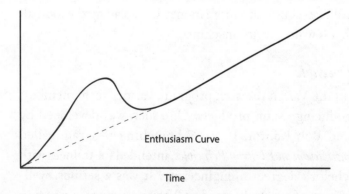

Reprinted from *NSPI Journal*, January 1960.

The introduction of a new technology is always accompanied by an over-abundance of hype and wild enthusiasm. Promoters make honestly but hastily-conceived promises that do not reflect the technology's real potentialities.

This first phase is followed by a period of general disillusionment, as people realize that the technology's impact is less than the ballyhooers promised. The faint of heart flee, and many new companies attempting to profit from the new technology close their doors.

This is taken as final evidence the new technology has failed.

Eventually, it becomes clear that, though the new technology won't solve all the world's problems, it nevertheless will provide considerable value. At this point the enthusiasm curve turns upward again as the "new" technology begins to take its rightful place in the field.

For the time being, enthusiasm for programmed instruction remained high, as evidenced by such events as the founding of NSPI in 1962.

Cover of Soldier's Handbook written for Company A (1943)

Technical Sergeant Carl Knelly, electronics genius

Ring announcer Mager introduces women's wrestling bout (1948)

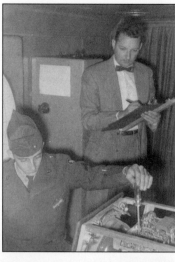

Observing a trainee during the three-hour performance test inside a radar van (1958)

Three-dimensional meter-reading practice items and carrying case

Automated fifty-item meter-reading testing machine

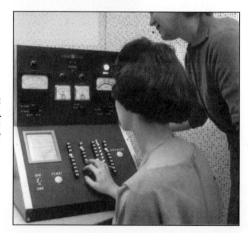

Mager with Dr. Toogie, ventriloquising during "The Perfect Banquet Speech" at the 1999 ISPI Conference

Backstage at Symphony Hall

Videotaping a presentation in the self-operated studio (1963)

Legs, legs, legs (1994)

After a book signing for Mager's first published novel aboard Holland America's Statendam cruise ship

See? It's really true!

thirteen

Visibility Sprouts

THE NATIONAL SOCIETY FOR PROGRAMMED INSTRUCTION (NSPI) was organized as an advocate for the new technology. Its mission was improving the effectiveness, efficiency, and elegance of programmed instruction. It changed its name in 1973 to The National Society for Performance and Instruction (still NSPI), when members realized that even elegant instruction wasn't the cure for all performance problems. The name was changed again in 1995, this time to The International Society for Performance Improvement (now ISPI), reflecting the fact that instruction is no longer viewed as the end in itself, but one of the possible means to the performance improvement goal. (Some of us still snicker that there must be a Permanent Name Change Committee lurking in the wings.)

Though there were, and are, other organizations purporting interest in the improvement of instruction and human performance, NSPI was most rigorously devoted to that goal. It was the organization with which one affiliated to meet and interact with leaders in the field and toilers in its vineyards.

Like most organizations, NSPI has an annual convention. For the first two years these were held in San Antonio, because its principal founder, Colonel Gabriel Ofeish, was stationed at Randolph Air Force Base. It was at these small (at first) conventions I first met some of the movers and shakers of the field—Lloyd Homme, Jim Evans, Tom Gilbert, Roger Kaufman, Susan Markle, Joe Harless, Bill Deterline, and others. They stood out because they were actively involved in advancing the field, rather than just lecturing about it. They were among the few who had actually written one or more programs. That, and their willingness to engage in free exchange of ideas, made them worth listening to and learning from. I always left these meetings spinning with new insights.

At the First Annual NSPI Conference in 1963, more than 650 attendees packed into the El Tropicano Hotel. Gabe Ofeish was the first NSPI president and proudly chaired the closing banquet from the ballroom podium. This was a big event for him, and rightly so.

Gabe had asked me to deliver the banquet speech, then told me I would speak on "Barriers to Innovation." It was difficult to defy this affable man who so loved giving orders, so I agreed. But it was even more difficult to avoid tweaking him on it. Here is the text of my speech:

"I'm sure you all noted the title of my talk in your program, so it wouldn't hurt to begin with an illustration of a Barrier to Innovation.

"Take Colonel Ofeish, for example . . .

"He was very generous to invite me to give this address and I appreciate it very much. But when he issued the invitation, it was done in two parts. In Part One, he invited me to talk on any subject I thought appropriate for an event such as this. In Part Two, he told me that the title of my talk would be 'Barriers to Innovation' and handed me a sheet of paper outlining several barriers I might wish to include in my discussion." *Pause*.

"Actually, the most *conforming* response I could make to the stimulus, 'Give a talk on Barriers to Innovation' would be to give a talk on Barriers to Innovation.

"On the other hand, the most *innovative* response I could make would be not only *not* to talk on Barriers to Innovation . . . but to refrain from giving a talk at all. In the interest of practicing what we preach, that's what I'll do. Thank you very much."

Then I sat down. Bedlam followed. The laughter was long and spirited—most of the audience knew Gabe and his propensity for orchestrating others' behavior. When the hall finally quieted, I stood up again—to a wave of groans. I continued, "For those who are interested, copies of my talk will be available on request," and sat down again. More bedlam.

By now Gabe had turned several colors and was in obvious pain— he'd lost control of the session and things weren't going at all as planned. Looking in his direction was too much to bear, so when all was quiet, I stood for a third time—to even louder groans. For a few minutes I commented on barriers to innovation but, as I'd already run out of prepared speech, I don't remember what I said.

Until that moment I had been an invisible member of the new NSPI organization. I'd earned a bit of visibility from the few papers I'd published, but few people recognized me on sight. That changed. Not only did I become visible, I was invited several times to present banquet addresses over the years. With one or two exceptions, these were eminently forgettable.

Dr. Dovard I. Joseph

One exception was a scam Joe Harless and I perpetrated on the membership in 1977, the year he was president. The program said the banquet speech, titled, "Yanks Know Nothing Whatsoever About Training," was to be offered by a Dr. Dovard I. Joseph, a noted somebody from Australia. Nobody had ever heard of him, but Harless had the show-biz moxie and dramatic ability to make the put-on work.

When banquet night arrived on April 15th and it was time to

introduce the speaker, Joe shame-facedly announced a last-minute change—some catastrophic event had prevented Dr. Joseph from appearing, and he had no substitute. As the crowd wondered how Harless would handle the problem, he intoned that he would assert his prerogative as president . . . and select a speaker from the audience.

The collective gasp was followed by nervous murmuring.

As he walked s-l-o-w-l-y among the tables with outstretched finger poised, he looked at each diner in turn. Everyone did his/her best to become invisible. Some turned their heads, some bent over to tie a shoelace, and others simply perspired. "Oh God, let it not be me!"

After what seemed an eternity, Joe whirled in my direction and shouted, "Bob Mager." The air expelled by the collective sigh of relief could have filled a hot air balloon.

It was my turn to prolong the tension. I rose and pretended panic as I walked slowly to the podium. By the time I reached the lectern and raised my head to speak, the hall was silent with anticipation. What could Mager possibly concoct in just a few seconds of preparation time? This is how I began:

"Have you ever had the nightmare that begins when you're sitting in an audience and someone suddenly introduces you as the featured speaker . . . and when you look down you find yourself completely naked? I have."

Heads nodded.

"Have you ever had the experience of attending a meeting, having been promised you won't be called on to say anything . . . only to be called on to say something?"

Vigorous nodding.

"It's happened to me more than once . . ." I paused before continuing, "and ever since, I've never gone anywhere unprepared."

On that line I reached into my coat and pulled out a few pages of notes. The applause was gratifying. I continued on for a few minutes, talking mostly about my, and Joe's, conviction that banquet speeches should be light and short, and that the last thing tired conference attendees needed after a week of serious presentations was . . . another one.

The deception was well received. But Joe and I still laugh that for years afterward more than a few attendees remained convinced that Dr. Dovard I. Joseph actually existed and the event was legitimate; they talked with satisfaction about how I had "gotten even" with Joe by being prepared. Some people will believe anything.

Even so, our light-hearted scam exposed the membership to a useful lesson—professional competitors can also be good friends, a fact that sometimes surprises people who should know better.

We later supported the Dovard I. Joseph myth by having "him" write letters to the NSPI Journal. Even today, people ask Harless if Mager is still angry with him for "doing that to him," and comment that Mager was a genius for being able to recover so cleverly. It's amazing what careful preparation . . . and rehearsals . . . can accomplish.

As I said, it was a great scam.

fourteen

Paris Calls

D URING THE SUMMER OF 1963, I had a visit from two interesting people. One was the managing director of a worldwide consulting firm based in Paris. The other was A. Robert Taylor, a sophisticated, savvy, and energetic man who had earned his bones—and then some—in the executive search and selection enterprise after a successful career as a Human Resources VP. These two gentlemen had traveled from Paris to (a) check me out, and (b) determine whether I'd be interested in joining their new venture as technical director. Their plan was to establish a consulting firm—Learning Systems Institute—offering programmed instruction solutions to companies in half a dozen European countries. (We were still in the initial rise of the normal enthusiasm curve described a few pages back.)

Bob Taylor described the performance problems and training situation in Europe and tried to convince me I'd be just the person to help provide solutions. After a lengthy discussion, I took my visitors to dinner at a well-known Palo Alto restaurant, where they received a taste of American "sophistication." When the managing director asked the waitress which wine she recommended, she nudged him in the shoulder with an elbow and said, "Take the red—it's good and cold." After that gargantuan gaffe, I was sure the deal was off. Fortunately, I was wrong. Whew!

If I accepted the offer, it would entail a move almost halfway around the world to an alien culture. My family and I teetered on the razor blade of indecision for some time. Finally, desperate for input, I followed a suggestion to talk with Dr. Ernest Hilgard, Stanford professor of education. He was only a mile or two away, so I asked for a meeting. He graciously agreed.

My main concern, I explained to him, was that if I moved to France I'd be out of sight, and touch (e-mail and fax didn't yet exist), and might not be able to find a job on returning to the USA. He counseled that nothing was certain, but thought the move would help, rather than hinder, my career. That did it; my wife and I decided to take the plunge. Another whack, this time landing me halfway around the world.

During the fall of 1963 we sailed to Paris (LeHavre, actually) by way of the S.S. France. It was a grand ship and gave our two boys a taste of the elegant life. Children were not allowed into the dining room for dinner, of course (an eminently civilized custom), but the boys didn't care. They had their own dining room and access to a large, well-equipped playroom, complete with nannies and food service.

The pleasant passage was followed by a difficult beginning. More than culture shock had to be survived. Our furniture wouldn't arrive for six weeks, my office wouldn't be ready for three weeks, and the villa we'd rented couldn't be occupied for almost a month. We had no choice but to camp out in a small French hotel. On the top floor, of course, just under the roof. During those weeks, the top of a steamer trunk became my office; a borrowed portable typewriter served as my office equipment. My French was mostly non-existent—a few tattered memories from slogging my way through *Les Trois Mousketaires*. So much for a whiz-bang beginning in a foreign culture.

Nonetheless, the work was challenging. I spent most of my time traveling by train from one country to another, trying to remember how to say "please" and "thank you" in the upcoming language, reviewing notes about customs to observe, and thinking about the forthcoming project.

Before the enterprise could become fully functional, we needed a few people who could be trained to develop programmed instruction. Where to look? How to advertise? Fortunately, the wisdom of Peter Pipe surfaced once again. "Programming is writing, and journalists write," he said. "If, at the end of the day, you want words on paper, hire journalists, not educators." That was good advice. Still is. When interviewing candidates, my first question became, "Can you show me something you've written? Anything. Letters, fiction, reports, grocery lists . . . " The notion was that if they hadn't written anything in the past, they wouldn't be comfortable with or good at a writing-intensive job with us.

The projects themselves were challenging, but not because the problems were difficult to solve. The challenge was all too often how to inform clients their problem couldn't be solved by instruction—programmed or otherwise. The European environment was considerably more formal than our own, so such messages had to be crafted with a great deal of tact.

In London, for example, I visited a large engineering consulting firm that wanted us to program the accounting portion of their training for newly hired engineering consultants. It seemed the instructor of that four-hour block wasn't very good at making accounting principles clear to the trainees. Hence the request for a programmed solution. That sounded reasonable, but a few questions made it clear that the proposed program was unnecessary. The new-hires not only didn't need to know anything about accounting, they'd damned well better not even *pretend* to know anything about accounting. Company policy forbade engineering consultants from dabbling in accounting; if it looked as though a client needed accounting assistance, the consultants were expected to call the home office.

Analysis needed

And so it went. After meeting with just a few potential clients I'd become painfully aware of the need for a screening device to filter client requests. It seemed like a slam dunk: Clients asked for instruction to solve their problems, and we had instruction to sell, so it seemed like an easy match. But it wasn't. When clients identified a problem involving any human performance, they always seemed to conclude that instruction was the remedy. And why not? It was how people everywhere in the world thought. The mantra seemed to be: If they're not doing what they should be doing, train 'em. No need to find out if they already knew how, or if something else prevented the desired performance.

This was how the world thought about the issue of training in 1964–65. Corporations had Training Departments, and training was what they delivered. Not solutions to problems—but training. Almost all perceived or imagined aberrations in human performance were "solved" by training. Period. That mindset is obsolete now, though it is still practiced. (Sigh.)

Had Learning Systems Institute not been an ethical enterprise, we could have provided training whenever it was requested. Life would have been easier and far more profitable. But our goal was to serve clients, not to provide worthless "solutions." Our need for a screening mechanism intensified. I dreamed about an algorithm to help clients determine whether they'd guessed right or wrong about training as the solution to their problem, something that wouldn't require us to invent tactful ways of saying, "Training won't help your situation one damn bit!"

My initial approach was to list conditions that would influence the recommendation of a training program versus something else. "How big is the population of trainees?" Too few students meant programmed instruction wouldn't be economically feasible, no matter how strong the need. "How much lead time is available?" Programming took time, and short lead time mitigated against using that technique. "Do they already know how do what you want them to do?" was also included—no point in teaching what they already knew.

My next step was to arrange the screening questions, in order of priority. For example, questions about the number of potential trainees and lead time came first. Unless the right conditions prevailed, there was no need to proceed to the questions that followed.

This was the beginning of what turned out to be the performance analysis procedure. After returning to the U.S., I enlisted Peter Pipe to collaborate on a book we eventually called *Analyzing Performance Problems*. It was published in 1970.

Teaching the test

On the one hand, we had companies clamoring for programmed instruction . . . but in the academic world resistance to change was as strong as ever. At a boys' junior high school in Genoa, Italy, we conducted a demonstration pitting programmed instruction against the traditional classroom methodology. One algebra class was selected to serve as the experimental group (programmed instruction or PI) and another as the control group (traditional instruction).

We wrote the first draft in English, translated it into French, conducted tryouts and revisions in that language, then trans-culturated the revised French version into Italian. Does that make your head hurt? It did ours, too, but we persevered until it was time to conduct the tryout.

By the time we arrived in Genoa for the tryout, we already had one strike against us—as soon as the teacher for the PI group was selected, he was branded a traitor to the school and shunned by his colleagues. The experiment began in that environment.

During a later visit to check on progress, I stepped into the control group classroom. Much to my astonishment, the teacher was *teaching the test!* The teacher would chant, "The answer to number three is A," and the students would chant back, "The answer to number three is A."

Angry at how our "experiment" was being undermined, I stormed to the headmaster's office and recounted my tale of woe. "Mister _____ is teaching the test!" I wailed. The headmaster looked at me as though I'd gone mad, but called for the teacher to join us. The conversation went something like this:

Headmaster:	"Is it true you are teaching the test?"
Teacher:	"Yes, of course!"
Headmaster:	"And why are you teaching the test?"
Teacher (Proudly):	"Because *I* was selected to uphold the honor of the school against programmed instruction."

Whereupon the headmaster looked in my direction, shrugged his shoulders, and said, "*See?*"

The programmed instruction group still performed better than the group rote-taught the test. Even so, the episode in Genoa pounded another nail into the conviction that effectiveness and efficiency are lower in priority than people pretend they are. In other words, all is not as it seems—or alleged.

I suppose it would be comforting to think that events such as these occur only in the Italian hinterlands. Not even close. Turf-protecting events are found everywhere; no country is immune from the fervent desire to protect the status quo.

Culture shock lives

The European experience was a large, and sometimes painful, growth experience, mainly because of the challenge of blending into cultures so different from our own . . . while trying to do meaningful work. I found it difficult to work in two or three cultures every week. I found it hard to formulate tactful ways to inform the client that instruction wouldn't help. I found it especially difficult to keep from blurting out an obvious "solution" before understanding whether the client was actually interested in solving the problem. Many were not. Hidden agendas were everywhere.

Sometimes it seemed as though the entire country conspired to prevent us from doing an honest day's work. When the electric typewriter we'd leased for my office finally was delivered, and I asked that it be plugged in and turned on, I was told, "Oh, no, no, no, monsieur. I'm just the delivering man. The plugging-in man will come tomorrow." (Why not plug it in myself? Don't ask.) Exasperating. When a truck arrived to deliver the dining room table and chairs we'd purchased, the table was unloaded. Period. I asked about the chairs.

"The chairs will be delivered on the "fragile" truck," I was told, with the usual Gallic shrug. As promised, the chairs arrived on the "fragile" truck only a few days later.

When I grumbled about the strangling bureaucracy, I was told—more than once—"Just wait. In twenty years America will be suffering from it, too." Unfortunately, they were absolutely right. The world is slowly strangling in red tape.

When it was time to arrange for a work permit, my secretary called the Préfect de Police to ask what documents I would need for my interview.

"Oh, no, no, no, Madame. First, you must come here, and *then* we will tell you what documents he must bring." Another half-day wasted.

Shopping was also a challenge. Breakfast cereal? Shrug. Catsup? Scowl. I soon developed the habit of smuggling two or three bottles of catsup in my briefcase when returning from trips to London. (I won't even mention what the French thought about people who squirt catsup onto their food.) But it was fun to shop in the village where we lived . . . where wine was thirty-nine cents a bottle.

On the bright side, trains ran on time, the food was excellent, and the people charming. More important, the medical system was superb.

When my younger son was whisked to the hospital with a serious malady, the care was instant, attentive, and first-rate. Almost without charge—even for foreigners. The entire bill for several days of hospital care came to 459 French francs—about $92.00.

The European experience wasn't all hard work and tears. Sometimes it was just embarrassing. My French was sketchy at best, and I still suffered from culture shock, but I jumped in and did the best I could, often to hilarious results. One day I was so busy at my desk I simply ignored the ringing telephone. Soon, I could hear our French-only receptionist tromping toward my office on the squeaky wood floor. Bursting into the office, she said, "You are here!"

"Oui," I replied, continuing my work.

"Why don't you answer your phone?" she demanded, again in French.

In perfect French, I responded, "Mon cheval est mouillé!" (my horse is wet!). It was the only phrase I could think of at the moment, learned that very morning from one of my boys' French primers. After that, I always tried out new phrases on her as I exited the creaky elevator on my trek to the office. We became fast friends—no doubt because of my entertainment value.

The most embarrassing incident, however, occurred during a dinner party at a posh restaurant. I asked the location of the rest room, which opened right onto the main dining room. On entering, I couldn't find the light switch, so I leaned out and called, "Ou est le lit?" thinking I had asked, "Where's the light switch?" After the laughter died down, I was told where it was. On returning to the table I was informed that I had asked, "Where's the bed?" Oh well.

My fractured French also saved me one day while driving my mini-car along the Champs Elysées. A French policeman stopped me and loosed a tirade too fast for me to understand. When he stopped to come up for air, I leaned my head out and said, "Vous parlez Français trés bien, monsieur." (You speak French very well, sir.) That stopped him cold, after which he could only shake his head, probably wondering what else he could expect from a crazy American.

He waved me on.

Spark Plugs 'R Us

Shortly after the Genoa boys' school "experiment," an opportunity presented itself that allowed me to practice what I was learning about the yet-unnamed performance analysis. Interestingly, the assignment had nothing whatsoever to do with instruction, programmed or otherwise. But it was this experience that sharpened my perception of how seriously the work environment can impact job performance and learning.

I was asked to perform a review of a spark plug factory in a charming village in central France. The factory had recently been converted from felt hats to spark plugs, and the managing director was concerned that the workers, mostly farm-raised women, would be less satisfied wrestling forty-pound boxes of spark plugs than needle and thread. (He needn't have worried; these women were no strangers to heavy lifting and found making spark plugs more to their liking than sewing felt hats.)

Because there had been reason to make the factory conversion happen as rapidly as possible, the managing director had sent a chemical engineer from Paris to set up the production line. Time was of the essence and there wasn't any choice. Though this engineer had no experience at this task, he dug in and did the best he could. And his best was none too shabby. By the time I arrived, they were making high quality spark plugs, and the women periodically burst into song at their work stations.

Not being familiar with principles of production flow, this engineer had set up the production line according to his version of "logical." He began by placing the larger pieces of machinery into available spaces, then tucked the smaller pieces into whatever empty spaces remained. "Is that an empty space over there in the corner? Fine. We'll put a drill press there." "Is that chair not being used? Good. Let Michelle sit on it."

As you might expect, the product traveled a rather convoluted path on its journey through the plant. In addition, a number of work stations were less than effectively designed. For example, because of the let's-use-the-chairs-we-happen-to-have principle, some workers were required to hold their hands too high or droop their heads too low while working, leading to painful necks and backs long before the end of their shifts. Because of the tuck-it-where-you-find-a-space principle of machine placement, workers had to be careful not to bump into one another as they moved boxes of plugs back and forth through the plant.

It wasn't difficult to identify any number of inefficiencies in machine placement, as well as job design and other ergonomic errors. For example, a long ceramic furnace had been installed just inside the entrance to one factory building—the wrong way around. As a result, raw materials had to be trucked into the factory all the way to the other end—the front end—of the furnace, while items coming out of the furnace had to be trucked all the way back to arrive at the next production point.

Was this an unusual situation? Far from it. That's why instruction should never be prescribed before analyzing the circumstances leading someone to say, "They need training." No matter where one goes in the world of work, one can find these and other job design errors which, if corrected, will make the work easier, more efficient, less tiring or painful, and/or safer—without requiring any training at all.

From then on I began seeing obstacles and mismatches everywhere I turned. I'd walk down the street and see a street vendor who could sell more products if he rearranged his wares. I'd note the inefficiency of using live ticket-takers in the French subway when an automated turnstile would hasten travelers on their way. (When I asked about that practice, I learned it was a way for the French government to provide gainful employment for pensioners. Oops! I'd jumped to a fine conclusion from a faulty premise.) As mentioned earlier, I saw obstacles to learning in every classroom and every textbook. Why didn't others see what I saw? Perhaps they did, but were far more relaxed about the disjoints than I.

Translators aren't interpreters

On several occasions, I had to make a presentation through a simultaneous interpreter. It is a humbling experience revealing how badly we communicate, even when speaking English to English-speaking audiences.

Typically, the interpreter assembled her portable booth at the back of the classroom, strung wires and headsets, and otherwise prepared for two-way language communication. I, for example, would speak in English, and the interpreter would exchange my words for those in the target language, while at the same time trans-culturating vocabulary and examples. All in real time!

Unless you speak the target language (and why use an interpreter if you do?), your success or failure is entirely in her hands. In plain language, if she doesn't like you, or if you piss her off, or treat her like furniture, you're dead. All she has to do is relax her vigilance to make a shambles of your presentation. Treat her right, though, and your success is all but assured.

A good interpreter can save your hide in other ways. For example, when I was asked to conduct a seminar for South American bankers in Washington, D.C., I met with the interpreter over breakfast before the meeting (by then I'd learned that not to do so could be the kiss of death). It was a good thing I did. She indicated that customs followed by South Americans during seminars were a bit different from ours. She explained:

"You'll present your first lecture, after which everybody will get up and leave the room."

"W-h-a-a-t?"

"Yes. They will go somewhere down the hall and caucus."

"Caucus?"

"Yes. They will discuss, and possibly argue, about what you told them. They will then return to the classroom, and someone will stand up and report. You will then be invited to deliver your next lecture."

Which is exactly what happened. Imagine how you'd feel if you didn't know what was coming, and suddenly your entire audience got up and left!

Fortunately, someone had taken me aside and confided the etiquette of dealing with interpreters. That kindness allowed me to be well-received where others—brilliant though they may have been—failed. Here's what you need to know:

First, never refer to an interpreter as a translator. *Translators* are highly skilled people who exchange the words of one language for those of another. That's difficult enough. *Interpreters*, on the other hand, do that and more; they select words, phrases, expressions and examples that will make your meaning clear in the target language and culture . . . and they do it in real time.

Second, always refer to your interpreter by name. It's common courtesy. If you're not sure how to pronounce it, ask. She'll be flattered by your interest.

Third, *always* try to arrange *private* time with your interpreter before your presentation. This will signal your respect for her as a person, give her a chance to hear the analogies and special terminology you will be using, and let her become accustomed to the sound of your voice and pronunciations. It can save you from certain death. While meeting with an interpreter in West Berlin, she explained that Germans reserve the word "behavior" to refer to the behavior of lower animals, not including humans. That single insight was enough to save me a great deal of embarrassment.

Humor can be another trap. What's funny in one culture isn't necessarily funny in another. If you hope to get a laugh for your hilarious anecdote, allow the interpreter an opportunity to find words that will push your humor into the target language. Don't even think of trying to tell a funny story without pre-testing it with your interpreter. If you do, disaster lurks.

There was an important lesson to be gleaned from these experiences with interpreters: It's much easier to talk than to communicate. It's difficult enough to communicate in one's own language. But when an interpreter stands between you and your listener, the problem of "getting through" is magnified.

Experiences with interpreters helped improve my "getting through" skills, and my attempts to navigate several European cultures led me to a deep appreciation of the importance of testing my written work before publication. Ever since, I've not published anything that hasn't been subjected to extensive tryouts on the intended audience. They're not always easy on the ego, but they guarantee I'll be understood better than had the tryouts not occurred. Besides, wouldn't you rather find out what's wrong with your written and spoken communications *before* they go out into the world?

A mind stretcher

The European experience definitely stretched my mind, especially because work and travel spanned several countries and as many cultures. It was well worth the effort, though, as it reinforced the perception that performance problems are pretty much the same the world over. They're expressed in different languages and wrapped in different cultures, but they're the same. And why not? The laws of nature and principles of behavior are universal—they operate whether we like it or not. It's that insight that allowed me to enter totally unfamiliar environments (brewery, gold mine, spark plug factory, etc.), confident I could find a way to be of service.

Speedy Development

W HEN THE JOB AT LEARNING SYSTEMS INSTITUTE drew to
a close (along with LSI itself), it was clear I hadn't as
yet arrived at "Here," and wondered again where that
might turn out to be.

The bumpers nudged me back to the laboratory, this time to
Webster, New York, to head the Behavioral Research lab at Xerox. It
was late 1965, and several companies were toying with the idea of
entering the education business in one way or another. A common
first step was to establish a small research facility and peer over the
shoulders of the researchers.

Once again I was surrounded by physicists and engineers.

Approach-avoidance

The Xerox research program was two-pronged: One focused on
finding ways to measure approach-avoidance tendencies toward
instructional content, and the other on learning how to develop

instruction under the constraints of very short lead time.

The approach-avoidance research was headed by Dr. Bruce Bergum, with whom I had worked in El Paso. In one experiment, for example, he showed someone a slide depicting an object, then measured the degree of physiological attraction or repulsion experienced by the subject.

Another experiment repeated the procedure with spoken words. While the subject looked at a blank screen, a word was spoken into the earphones, the physiological responses were recorded, and the process was repeated with the next word. The equipment was sensitive enough to assess the approach-avoidance strength of single syllables.

Bergum learned to detect words and images that turned people on or off, and we envisioned that becoming a useful tool in the design of instruction. We looked forward to the day we could test our instruction and delete or modify the components that turned students off. By minimizing the unattractiveness of the material to be learned we were confident we could make attitude toward learning even more favorable.

It all seemed straightforward until his results revealed something unexpected. The psychological literature of the time alleged that the English word eliciting the greatest emotional response was a person's own first name. Bergum discovered that at that time in Rochester, New York, that word was *mink*. (Once again, all our subjects were employees' wives, mostly of corporate managers.) But that was then.

Speed development

The speed development work was my project, and it generated a fair amount of derision and snide remarks. My aim was to learn how to develop instruction in the shortest possible time, but in truth, nobody cared. As far as most were concerned, it was a non-issue. Nobody really cared how long it took to *develop* instruction; attention was focused almost entirely on *delivery* time. Teaching more in less time— that was the quest.

This shouldn't have been surprising, I suppose, in an environment where systematic development was thought to be unnecessary. "Winging it" in the classroom was considered not only acceptable, but a badge of honor—Macho-man at work. From there, it was inevitable that clients believed development, speedy or otherwise, to be a luxury they needn't afford.

Looking to the future, I thought I could see a time when systematic development would be taken seriously. I envisioned an instructional SWAT team called to action when time was of the essence in solving a performance problem; our graphic artist even drew sketches of a portable van in which the team might work.

We conducted experiments to discover the secret to "instant development." But circumstances turned it into a difficult quest. My team had their own projects to pursue and grumbled when I asked them to spend time on mine. Subject-matter "experts" assigned by management often weren't experts at all. They found it almost impossible to set aside their canned lectures and respond to questions peppered at them by the team. More troubling, we had a hard time finding performance problems requiring instruction—the target audience almost invariably knew whatever it was we "needed" to teach them.

When we ran out of company problems, we turned to the local school system, and were presented with a problem in map reading. We were told that fourth graders entered the map reading segment of the course with misconceptions, such as "Up is North, and down is South." It drove the teacher bananas. So we invited the teacher to play subject-matter expert and conducted a "speed run," during which the team quickly sucked her dry of information. This was the smoothest run of all. The SME reported being comfortable with the proceeding and wasn't stressed by the nature and frequency of the team's interruptions. Interestingly, we learned that the reason kids entered the fourth grade thinking that "up is North and down is South" was because *that's what they were taught in the first grade.* (Imagine what school might be like if the left academic hand knew what the right one was doing.)

In the end, we confirmed that shortening instructional development time was easily possible. And in those instances where analysis showed no instruction was needed, we "shortened" instruction time, in effect, to zero. Nobody was impressed. We also learned how difficult it is to expect instructors to adjust their instruction to fit individual students' needs.

Ten years later, I delivered a paper titled, "Instant Instructional Development" to the annual NSPI convention. The presentation was well received, but even then nobody much cared about reducing development time. (One reviewer of an earlier draft snidely commented: "Now they don't care whether the instruction works, as long as it's developed by Thursday.")

Shinichi Suzuki

One day, an unexpected visitor stepped into the Xerox lab. We were on his list of stops during his tour of the Fundamental Research Laboratory. His name was Shinichi Suzuki, the music teacher famous for teaching violin to very large groups of students. I jumped at this rare opportunity to question him about his methodology. Yes, he believed in teaching violin in groups (so large they filled a gymnasium) and had no shortage of competent violinists to prove the efficacy of his approach.

He stressed the importance of facing students with the purpose of the instruction from the very outset. In other words, first he had them pick up a violin and try to play. Only after they had actually experienced the problems of playing did he offer coaching designed to improve the performance. Topics like music theory were studied only after students had developed some facility with the instrument— only after students had enough skill to allow them to understand and make use of theory.

This was the same methodology used by my instructor, Charlie Tagawa, when I decided to learn to play tenor banjo a few years later. When I arrived for my first lesson, he tuned up my instrument, handed it to me, and said, "Let's play." I sat there with an expression screaming, "You've got to be kidding. Wot? No theory of banjo?" Didn't matter. Somehow, we played. First he allowed me to experience the purpose of the instruction—playing the banjo—then filled in the information gaps as we "played." We never strayed from the main purpose of the session: improving my performance.

The lesson is clear: Hands-on practice first, then theory. Give trainees something of the real world to relate theory information to. Don't try to get them to think in the abstract until you've given them something concrete to be abstract about.

Good grief! Let's get ON with it!

About the time I was working on the speed development research at Xerox, I was invited to the meeting of a task force in Washington, D.C., weasel word capital of America.

The self-imposed mission of the task force was to "do something" about vocational education. More specifically, to do something to inform vocational educators of current trends in instructional design. There was lots of talk at the meeting about what to do and how to proceed. Finally the talk turned to the idea of putting a book together articulating the principles of systematic instructional design, as well as about how such a thing might be accomplished and at what cost. But no one made a decision. Hands were wrung, wheels were spun, and it began to seem that every idea would lead to another round of fruitless discussion.

Finally, completely frustrated by the rising depth of the BS, I said, "Look. Give me five hundred dollars and I'll put the book on your desk in six months." Desperation will lead to that kind of careless talk. Surprisingly, the committee accepted the offer, promised a grant, and I went back to Xerox to write the book. That was the beginning of *Developing Vocational Instruction*.

Ken Beach, my chief technician at the time, agreed to collect examples while I drafted the book. Desmond Wedberg wrote a chapter listing current sources of instructional materials, and Ivor Davies crafted a Preface. David Cram, Bruce Bergum and Dick Lewis reviewed the manuscript. After revision, it was ready to send to the task force. They liked it, distributed it to their members, and arranged formal permission for me to publish it privately, which I did in 1967.

Because of the chapter listing available resources, it was out of date the minute it was published. Even so, it seemed to fill a need. That became clear years later when I begged the publisher to take it off the market. He refused; it was still selling. It was only much later, when publication of all my books was taken over by The Center for Effective Performance—bless them all—that I managed to make it happen. I promised CEO Seth Leibler I'd rewrite six of my other books (published together as the Mager Six-Pack) if he'd kill the book. He agreed—and kept his word. So did I.

Oops

After three-plus years in the Xerox lab, I made the mistake of turning down a management position, explaining that I'd rather stay in research for the present. It was more complicated than that, of course, so I'll just say that stance was out of tune with The Organization Man culture of the day. As a result of this, and other corporate no-nos, it was subtly made clear my presence was no longer required. I slunk off into the sunset . . . but fortunately, not without a destination.

sixteen

The Angle of Dangle

URING XEROX DAYS, a few toilers in the performance vineyard talked enthusiastically about learning to ride a unicycle. That sounded like an exciting challenge, so I bought one (no instructions included). As there were no unicycle instructors in sight, I tried to teach myself. Like a good little scientist, I made notes after every practice session, mainly to record progress. For a long time, there wasn't any. I'd get on, and fall right off. Bruises: 20, Progress: Zero.

Eventually, I learned to ride—and made an astonishing discovery. The reason I kept recording a lack of progress was that I had elected to use "distance of ride" as my progress measure. It seemed the natural thing to do. But for a long time, the distance recorded was zero inches. As I said, that was discouraging.

Once I learned to ride, I found I had been making progress all along, but didn't know how to recognize it. For example, as time progressed, the bruises on my legs moved from my ankles toward my crotch. The farther up my leg the bruises traveled, the closer I was to riding. When I began riding, a protractor under my arms provided another progress indicator—the more my balance improved, the smaller the angle between body and arms. This was the "angle of dangle" indicator—the better I got, the lower my arms got, until ultimately I could hold them in my lap.

Good instructions would have described these indicators and helped prevent the gloom cloud rising from my "no progress" chart. It was another important lesson: Don't let students practice on their own until you've taught them to recognize their own progress. "See? You only recorded twenty-seven bruises today instead of the forty-five you recorded yesterday. You're making good progress!" At the same time, downplay the distance yet to travel on the road to competence. Avoid idiotic comments such as, "Oh, sure, now you can play Chopsticks, but you've a l-o-n-g way to go before you're ready for the concert stage."

Banjo on my knee

Concurrently, an opportunity presented itself for an informal experiment in instructional sequencing. It happened after a chance meeting with a high school student who gave blue-grass banjo lessons. He charged seventy-five cents per lesson. I explained what I had in mind and told him that I would pay him twice that—as long as he did it my way. The minute he insisted on doing it his way, we would go back to seventy-five cents. That proved sufficient motivation to enlist his cooperation. He didn't know what he was in for. (This occurred a few years before the tenor banjo lessons from Charlie Tagawa.)

We sat facing one another and began. I asked questions and he responded. I asked another question, and he responded. I knew he wasn't used to this procedure and reassured him frequently that he was doing just fine.

Before long I realized the environment was getting in the way of learning. When I sat facing him, I had a good view of his hands, but I had to turn my head to see his fingering the way I was seeing my own. When I moved to sit next to his right side, that environmental obstacle disappeared and we sailed along.

Two things happened. First, I learned so much so fast (compared to my previous attempts at music) that I practiced during every available moment. I had so much fun and found the progress so rewarding I could hardly wait for the next opportunity to practice. Second, my serious practicing improved my skill faster than that of my teacher's other students. At that point, he seemed to forget I was a beginning student and started treating me like a colleague. "Here," he'd say, "Let's play this," forgetting I was a novice without any idea of what he wanted me to do. Naturally, I couldn't keep up. The summer ended in the nick of time, as did the experiment.

This was the first time I'd experienced the learner-controlled technique as a student, and was pleased to find how exhilarating it could be. No wonder motivation doesn't have to be a problem.

Caution: Juggler approaching

Before leaving Xerox, the random finger of fate poked again when a box containing half a dozen juggling balls materialized. Aha! Another opportunity to keep in touch with the world from the learner's point of view. It was time to try another new skill. After developing a rudimentary ability (i.e., I could keep three balls flying for a few seconds without dropping any), I wrote a list of fourteen instructions with which to teach someone else the same skill. When tested on two people, the instructions managed to teach them the three-ball juggle in a little over one hour.

That was far too long. With trial and error, I was able to pare the list to eight instructions. That worked much better. But something was still wrong. The instructions taught the skill, but there were still too many words.

The solution was embarrassing. Three-ball juggling seemed so simple it hadn't occurred to me to be explicit about what I was trying to accomplish, that is, to state my objective. As soon as I did, five more instructions could be deleted. The initial absence of an explicit objective had lured me to the false assumption that I'd have to teach *all* the juggling steps. But there is, after all, only one "new" idea to be grasped, assuming the objective is to juggle three balls—rather than to juggle expertly. Most people only need to be taught that one idea—they already have the other skills required.

As with the speed development experiments, I observed yet again the amount of "noise" present in most communications and instruction. The search for the simple is rewarded not only by instruction that works, but by instruction that works with elegance. My final list of instructions contained only three.

By now I was hooked. Making instruction work better than it had in the past was an intriguing quest. Aha! Maybe that's what I wanted to do when I grew up. But the thrill of research had waned; rather than add grains of insight to the growing pile of knowledge, I now wanted to make a difference by putting knowledge to work. That suggested focusing on models of exemplary instruction and extracting the essence of their success.

There was no shortage of success models, if one was willing to look outside the classroom for examples. Fortunately, I had discovered yet another gold mine from which lessons about learning might be extracted. . . .

seventeen

Learning by Mail

O VER TIME I HAD BECOME MORE AND MORE CURIOUS about how things were done—and how doers learned to do what they did. That curiosity about how things are done has caused me on more than one occasion to be caught staring at people as they work. It's always been a treat to be allowed into someone's place of business to see how things happen. For example, Peter Pipe and I once accepted an opportunity to ride an elevator ten thousand feet below the surface of the earth in a South African gold mine. (Note: That far down one is pretty close to the Devil, which is why the temperature is about 120 degrees Fahrenheit and air conditioning is required.) We also spent time learning how breweries operated, and watched people work in a dynamite factory (very carefully).

Unfortunately, it isn't practical to visit every interesting factory, any more than it is practical to enroll in every course that seems intriguing. I found, however, a terrific alternative—the correspondence course. I've taken advantage of several over the years, ranging in quality from superb to abysmal, so in addition to the main subjects, each taught me something about how, and how not, to structure effective instruction.

A new career possibility?

My first experience occurred in 1957 during a lull at the research unit in El Paso. After scouring magazine ads looking to learn something new, three of us pooled our money and mailed in the required twenty-five dollars for a course in casemaking. The ad promised detailed instructions and enough materials with which to construct three cases. These would be custom-made cases with fitted and lined interiors, useful for housing anything from a piccolo to an engine. The cases themselves would be constructed of plywood and covered in vinyl. Interiors could be lined with anything from vinyl to felt to plush. We mailed the envelope . . . and waited.

When the box arrived and we studied its contents, we were pleasantly surprised to find them true to the ad's promise. There was indeed enough material to make at least three cases (not including plywood), and the instructions were superb. At least two hundred small photos depicted every step of the process—only a complete klutz could fail to follow them to a successful case.

In spite of that, my colleagues soon lost interest and left me to proceed on my own. I made first one case, then another. Then, to my astonishment, someone asked me to make a plush-lined case to hold a long cigarette holder, as a present for a general. The finished product was handsome. The casemaking instructions were truly well-crafted.

My astonishment continued as a friend of a friend drove his car into our driveway one day and asked that I reupholster his car door. I told him I didn't know how to do that, but he persisted. So I reupholstered his car door.

A few cases later, a representative from El Paso Natural Gas Company called me to his office to talk about a case problem. I was flattered. When he told me he wanted to order four hundred fitted cases, I threw in the towel. This was supposed to be a part-time hobby, after all, not a growing business. Unknowingly, I had tapped into a strong niche market! Many people wanted custom cases to house their special, and often expensive items, and I could have made a comfortable living serving their needs. That wasn't on the agenda, however. Since then I've made several cases, but only for myself, my puppets, and my family. Puppets? Read on.

Ventriloquism

Like most kids, I looked at the "Lemme out" magazine ads and fantasized myself a famous ventriloquist making all kinds of things talk. Too, I was curious about how the illusion was created. An opportunity presented itself when, in 1969, I bought a ventriloquial correspondence course, and bought a used vent figure (if you call them "dummies" they'll find ways to get even) from a retiring ventriloquist. (At the time, I had no idea the Davenport vent figure would be a collector's item.) I began reading and practicing the exercises.

The course wasn't badly constructed, but it was slow going. Practice was difficult without a video monitor for feedback. There was a source of immediate feedback for lip control practice (a mirror), but none for manipulation practice (making the puppet move as though alive). I'd sit at home with a puppet on my knee trying to practice, talking to myself, and feeling silly. It just wasn't working. Though the family said they did in fact hear the puppet talking, *I* didn't. I developed no confidence at all in what I later discovered was a growing skill. (Remember the unicycle episode where I selected the wrong indicator of progress?) Things improved when I began practicing in front of our video camera and could watch the results on the monitor.

Later, at the urging of a ventriloquist I met at a Magicians' Convention, I entered their vent contest with a borrowed right-handed puppet I'd been introduced to only the night before. As there were only five contestants, they pleaded with me to fill in as the sixth. Frantic, I practiced in front of the bathroom mirror while improvising a short skit. (The act involved having stage hands push me onto the stage while I resisted, pretending to be scared mute. During this time, the exasperated puppet encouraged the audience to try to applaud me out of my "coma" and talk.)

To my amazement, I won the contest and was more than mildly astonished when a psychiatrist approached me from the audience. He praised me for producing ". . . the best depiction of a catatonic I've ever seen." Gee, thanks a lot!

Even so, I still felt silly when practicing or performing. It was several years later that I found a book revealing the all-important bit of information I had been lacking: ventriloquists themselves can *never* hear the illusion! No matter how skillful they become at making the puppet talk, they can never avoid hearing in their own head the voices they're making for the puppet. Well, of course! It was suddenly obvious. But such obvious facts are often not obvious to the struggling learner. Knowing that critical fact made it possible for me to develop confidence and quickly learn to act as though the voices were being produced by the puppets themselves.

This experience gave me insight into the reasons instruction offered by subject matter experts often is flawed and difficult to understand. People highly knowledgeable in a subject are very likely to leave out critical pieces of information when offering explanations. It's best, therefore, always to question experts closely when using them as a source of information. They don't deliberately withhold information; it's just that they learned those critical bits so long ago they're often unaware of what they're doing or take those bits for granted.

When I took banjo lessons from Charlie Tagawa during the seventies, I would periodically grab his wrist and ask, "Why did you do that?" Often, his reply was, "Do what?" His skills were and are so polished he's hardly aware of what his fingers are doing—maybe they don't tell him, thinking he has no need to know.

To highlight this point, an old book on ventriloquism instructed that, to make the distant voice (from behind a curtain, a door, inside a suitcase, etc.), the reader should "Roll your tongue back to your diaphragm and slowly open your mouth." (*Don't* try that at home, or anywhere else. You might strangle yourself.) This example illustrates why we shouldn't let experts write instructional material without testing the materials before publication.

During 1975 I attended the first annual ventriloquist convention at the Drawbridge Hotel in Fort Mitchell, Kentucky. As a complete stranger to the group, I entered the contest in the senior division against 32 other contestants. The banquet hall was filled with more than four hundred ventriloquists. Because the "stage" consisted of nothing more than a few risers, there were only makeshift curtains behind which contestants could congregate and prepare. So contestants lined up against the wall of the banquet hall, inching forward as each concluded his or her six-minute act. With thirty-two senior contestants (professionals are mixed in with the amateurs) and almost as many in the junior (under sixteen) division, it was a l-o-n-g evening. (At six minutes per act, you can do the math.)

In spite of the heavy competition—and a serious case of nervousness—I won.

That taught me there's more to winning than skill. A substantial number of contestants were excluded from the list of finalists because they chose to preach rather than entertain (lots of ventriloquists use puppets in Sunday School). Following the rules matters: Others were rejected because they exceeded the time limit.

Two of five finalists lost out because they decided to "wing it" with an unrehearsed six-minute segment of a skit different from the one with which they qualified. But preparation counts. These professional vents were more skilled than I—but bombed because they were unprepared. The other two finalists were excellent ventriloquists, but their material consisted of a string of unrelated jokes—mine consisted of a skit with a story line. I won the trophy. When people ask me to describe my peak life experiences, this is the one I talk about first.

(By the way, the winner of the Junior Division trophy was Jeff Dunham, a wonderful vent who has since made many appearances on the Tonight Show with Johnny Carson, and later Jay Leno, and performs regularly in comedy clubs throughout the U.S.)

Locksmithing

By far the best course I've taken in my entire life was a correspondence course on locksmithing. I found the ubiquitous ad urging me to "Be a Locksmith" in an issue of Popular Mechanics and sent away for the information. When the first few lessons arrived, I immediately dived in.

Expecting the course to begin with dreary expositions on the history of locks, or key appreciation, I was pleasantly surprised to learn that lesson number one was on how to pick a lock. A combination lock was provided (the kind often used on high school lockers) along with a suitable pick, and within ten minutes of beginning the course, I was deeply engrossed in practicing a fascinating skill.

At the end of the very first lesson, I was able to exclaim, "Hey, lemme show you how I can pick this lock!" A real feeling of accomplishment as a result of the first lesson, and I didn't even know anything about the history of pin tumblers.

The next lessons were also task-oriented, with time taken out to learn what I needed to know (the "theory") just before beginning to practice. And, after each lesson I could do something important to the final goal I couldn't do before.

The mechanics of the course were so motivating I once found myself writing a letter to the instructor: "Your advertising promised that your mailings are scheduled so I'll never be out of lessons, but I've been out of lessons now for three whole days. Hurry up and send more!"

How was this motivation accomplished? Three to five lessons were packaged into a booklet of instructions, and mailed in a box containing several two- by three-inch numbered brown envelopes, along with tools or parts. The instructions dictated when to open certain envelopes. Tearing the envelope open would reveal a key blank, or an Allen wrench, or a set of pins, which would be put to immediate use in a practice exercise.

But there was more. A constant stream of items arrived in the mail. I received a series of lock cores, with instructions to change the combination to the numbers given and return them to the instructor. I received a bag of combination locks with instructions to pick them open, tape them in place, and return them to the instructor. At one point I even received part of a car door and was told that the door-locking mechanism had a broken spring. I was instructed to make a new one, install it, and return it to the instructor.

Lesson sequencing was beautifully orchestrated. The first lesson plunged the student immediately into the most intriguing topic—lock-picking, after which the other high-interest skills and topics were seeded throughout the remainder of the course. The least interesting skills—paperwork tasks associated with the craft—were saved until the end, when the student could already smell the fresh ink on a diploma.

Truly a splendid example of instructional design and delivery. The entire course was built around the tasks to be mastered. Immediate practice of new skills led to growing confidence and eagerness to learn more. Feedback was built into the tasks being practiced (e.g., it was obvious whether you did or did not pick a lock open). Finally, theory was seeded in chunks just large enough to prepare for the practice to follow. In sum, the course was masterfully constructed to implement just about every principle of effective instruction (and that was back in the sixties).

Did it work? Did I learn anything useful? The big test came one day in the parking lot at Xerox, when a senior manager discovered he had locked himself out of his foreign sports car. *This*, I thought, donning my virtual cape, *is a job for Lock Man*, and offered to have a go. Having left my picks at home, I borrowed a tool kit from one of the techies in the group, selected a couple of pointy things, and popped the lock open within thirty seconds. (Somehow I forgot to tell my surprised colleagues that many car door locks hardly deserved to be called locks at all.) The satisfaction of that moment still lingers.

It was obvious through my experiences with correspondence courses that the secret of the success of a course is not shrouded in the theatrical skill of an instructor, nor in the sophistication of the media through which it is presented. The magic is in the degree to which the principles of effective instruction are implemented—instruction leading to the ability to perform useful skills, that provides relevant practice and feedback, as well as lessons sequenced to motivate the student rather than to satisfy tradition or instructor preference. With those ingredients in the instructional soup, success is all but guaranteed.

In sum

Periodically adopting the role of student has been a useful activity, heightening my sensitivity to obvious and subtle do's and don'ts of instructional design. Perhaps more important, an occasional stroll in the students' shoes reminds me of the vulnerability they often feel when faced with learning something new.

These correspondence courses sprinkled themselves throughout my life like cherries tossed onto a moving canal barge. I learned more through these course about how various instructional acts made learners feel than if I'd just referred to the research literature. Much more.

But, getting back to chronology (can a person be chronologically-impaired?), we'll return to the "there-to-here" narrative. Another whack was imminent.

eighteen

Life on the Edge

SHORTLY BEFORE I LEFT XEROX, Dr. John Flanagan, founder of the American Institutes for Research (AIR), had asked if I'd be interested in assisting with a major project he was undertaking in Palo Alto. After a meeting to discuss details, I decided to sign on. After years in a laboratory prying snippets of knowledge from Mother Nature, I was ready to put my experience to more practical use. I wanted to make a difference during my lifetime.

California, here we come—again!
So in 1968, my wife, our two sons (now 11 and 14), and I moved from snow-drenched New York back to tax-drenched California to begin the new adventure. Thinking this was where the "Here" of "from there to here" would finally screech to a stop, we began digging in—literally. Though the house we bought was new, it was still in bare-bones condition. We hired a contractor to build a pool and patio, and the boys and I constructed a deck and retaining wall. Pouring

concrete and constructing cinder block walls provided great late afternoon exercise for all. We had a small building designed and constructed a few feet from the house—office space upstairs for writing and such; workshop and darkroom on the ground floor for fun.

The resulting arrangement worked well enough, but something was missing. Frequent travel was by then wearing thin, and I longed for ways to reduce the time spent on an airplane. I even charted the number of trips per year. When the number dipped toward zero, I considered that year a success. When the line climbed toward the sky, I thought harder about taking action. What to do?

When asked to take on speaking assignments requiring air travel, I longed to be able to say, "How about if I send a short video presentation, and then you can open the microphones and phone line for questions and answers." That would save the client money and offer an opportunity to make use of "technology," all the while saving wear and tear on my anatomy.

To make this possible, I built a small video studio in one of the rooms of our office area. I constructed a four-camera set-up—two floor cameras, one overhead camera (to show documents and sketches), and one through which to project slides. To make it work, I sat at the console and switched cameras as I talked. That may sound like a lot of complex manipulation—and it was—but I was an old sound-effects man used to such joyful activity. Besides, I could practice as much as it took to get it right . . . and do it over as many times as needed without wasting anyone else's time.

(After one of my taped presentations was viewed by a military client, a Captain was sent to examine my rig. The client thought they might make cheaper videos themselves if their studio could be transformed into one operated by one person. It was amusing to watch the Captain as I demonstrated. Finally, he shook his head and concluded they didn't have enough people who could drive the equipment and talk at the same time.)

The project

In the meantime, I focused my attention on my assignment from Flanagan. His project—bankrolled by Westinghouse—involved the development of a complete objective-based public school curriculum in the basic subjects, spanning grades K-12, and tailored to the needs of the individual student. It was a giant undertaking. Flanagan assigned me to direct about thirty volunteer teachers on loan from their schools to write the instructional materials.

Each of the objective-based lessons was intended to include the instruction needed to accomplish its objective. Easier said than done. Though all the volunteer teachers tried to follow what was for them an unusual format, their traditional educational mindset created serious obstacles. In their world, one first presented subject matter, and then wrote test items to discern how much of that material students could reproduce—somewhat like throwing a handful of tacks to the floor and counting those landing point up. We, on the other hand, asked them to proceed according to a radically different paradigm: decide *in advance* how many tacks they wanted to have land point up and *only then* think about how to make that happen. That was like asking a composer first to decide how he/she wanted listeners to feel, and then write music to evoke that desired response—and revise it until it did.

Also, the teachers struggled to write objectives describing what students should be able to *do*, rather than what they should *know*. That took training, along with emotional and administrative support. Without that training, it would have been unreasonable to expect teachers to recognize—and delete—content irrelevant to accomplishing an objective. The standard school curriculum, after all, had been standard for a long time.

Another problem arose because the developers were teachers, not writers. As a result, a wide range of writing skill surfaced—some teachers wrote beautifully, many struggled, and the frequent rewrites slowed progress. All the teachers, however, were enthusiastic about creating a coherent school curriculum and worked hard at their tasks.

It was interesting to hear teachers from different disciplines coordinate content with one another and work to resolve unnecessary duplications. They frequently discovered topics taught in multiple courses and grade levels, (how to use a microscope, for example). (If all such duplications were removed from the 12-year curriculum, it might be reduced to six years or so. Smirk.)

A year later, a budget crunch crept out of the woodwork. The project was progressing nicely, but consuming resources faster than expected. This was disappointing, especially because we were blessed with dedicated teachers and an engaging project. To ease the financial burden, I volunteered to reduce my work load to one day a week. The act wasn't entirely altruistic. I'd suddenly realized I was getting enough calls for consulting to suggest that it might be the time to dare to strike out on my own. After brow-furrowing discussions with my wife, we decided it was. When John Flanagan agreed to provide a safety net—one day of work each week, I established Mager Associates in 1969.

Thus began another adventure. Risky? Sure. But maybe now I would find out what I wanted to be when I grew up.

Going ape

While the entrepreneurial adventure took shape, a mischievous pinball flipper swatted me on the behind. Walking past the local pet shop one day, I noticed two young gibbon apes huddling together in the window. Could I just stroll by and leave these lonely orphans behind? The look in those soulful eyes said, "No way!" So I took them home in a cardboard box and presented them as a surprise Valentine's Day present to my wife. It was definitely a surprise.

Suddenly we were the "parents" of two six-month old gibbons who could leap twenty feet from a standing start. I had to build a cage—and fast. Soon one wall of the family room—floor to ceiling—became home for the gibbons. They were fun to have around, except when they were let loose during cage-cleaning day. (We never did solve the mystery of how they managed to poop on the *underside* of the furniture.)

There's a point to this story. Invariably, one of the apes would rattle their aluminum food dish during the climax of a TV program. Irritated, we'd turn in their direction, wave our arms, and shout, "Stop that!" That just made them do it again. To stop the racket, someone would eventually go to the kitchen and get them a banana.

Think about this interchange from the apes' point of view. Rattling their dish led to attention, funny shouting noises, and a banana. Highly rewarding, wouldn't you say? We could almost hear one saying to the other, "Hey, Tiny, watch me get a banana." It was never clear whose behavior was being engineered by whom.

Now translate this type of interchange to the classroom. When allegedly inappropriate behavior is rewarded by attention—scowls, funny shouting noises, giggles from classmates, etc.—that's rewarding, too. Under such circumstances, why should anyone expect the "problem" behavior to stop?

When the apes grew to the size of King Kong, we knew it was their turn to move. We hadn't signed up, but ape owners mysteriously become members of the Simian Society. We learned through their newsletter that one of our little friends was a rare breed. On learning this fact, the San Francisco Zoo said they'd be thrilled to have him and sent curators to move him to his new home. The other was gladly received by the San Jose Zoo, where he was quickly adopted by one of the older apes. When we went to visit, we knew he still remembered us because he peed on us through the bars of the cage. No doubt he meant well, but some gestures of friendship we can do without.

Into the abyss

Apes or no, I suddenly found myself looking over the edge of a cliff. I had just started my own business, but wasn't yet a businessman. I needed to attract clients to make the business prosper, but I wasn't a marketer. It was sink or swim in a competitive world. What was I thinking?

When I stopped feeling anxious long enough to inventory my assets, I realized I wasn't starting at Square One—I already had several strong allies. My wife was an accomplished typist and bookkeeper and graciously agreed to handle the office work—in addition to the two boys, the house, the garden, and the dog. That, by itself, provided an enormous advantage. The day a week at AIR provided a small financial cushion. Bill Deterline, president of a Bay Area consulting firm, General Programmed Teaching (GPT), offered to retain my consulting services—another small cushion.

The initial "marketing program" for the new enterprise consisted entirely of the book *Preparing Instructional Objectives* serving as a tireless sales "staff" working to keep my name in sight. Not much of a marketing program, but better than nothing. I was off and running—trepidaciously.

Those entering the world of the entrepreneur know the feeling of wondering where the next meal might come from. Will the phone ring? Will the mail bring a request for services? Often, this feeling of insecurity will lead to accepting any project that even smells like a paying job. Fortunately, the phone rang, and I found myself conducting workshops and seminars for school faculties, and for organizations as far away as South Africa. Industry consulting assignments included requests for seminars, workshops, keynote addresses, and performance problem-solving. These allowed me to meet interesting people and try out new ideas. Usually, they led to a referral or two.

It soon became clear that speaking engagements were not cost-effective: Because of the way my head worked, I couldn't do a "canned" presentation, and I certainly wouldn't just show up and "wing it." As a result, I spent too much time preparing and rehearsing for these one-time-only events for them to be economically viable.

I soon learned to recognize unsuitable assignments just by listening to the opening comments. For example, "We're a non-profit organization . . ." usually meant, "We want you do something free of charge." I also turned away most short lead-time requests. Speaking requests from schools were well-meant, but often I found them demeaning. "What would you like me to accomplish?" I'd ask. "Oh, you know. Just come and do your thing." Or, "Why are you inviting me?" often led to, "We haven't had you yet." I stopped accepting those requests as soon as I could afford to. Besides, I saw no hope of ever having a positive effect. As a prominent person once said: "Changing the education system is like trying to change the temperature of the ocean by pissing in it."

Hidden agendas are everywhere

Consulting during those days with Bill Deterline at GPT added to my education. Bill was a creative, well-educated, energetic guy who involved himself in a variety of projects and activities (including fiction-writing later in his career). He even accepted government projects, something I refused to do after discovering the pain associated with that process.

Working with Deterline confirmed yet another universal truth. For example, he had landed a hospital contract to produce training modules for nurse's aides. The modules were intended to teach entry-level skills such as turning a patient over in bed, assisting with first ambulations, and so on. Once the modules were ready for tryout, he requested the assistance of several nurse's aides from the contracting hospital. The aides appeared at the appointed time, worked through the modules, and completed the proficiency tests.

Lo and behold, their scores were almost uniformly perfect—and much too good to be true. Deterline smelled a rat. On questioning the "aides," he learned they weren't aides at all. They were all registered nurses pretending to be aides. Why? To uphold the reputation of the hospital—to keep the hospital from looking bad—they'd been told to disguise themselves as aides. (Remember the Genoa experiment?)

The experience underlined yet again that turf protection is often considered more important than effectiveness or efficiency. If a desired outcome is to be achieved, hidden agendas must always be considered.

"Fuzzies" abound

Publication of the objectives book in 1962 had caused a vexing problem to sprout like mold in a damp closet. As people struggled to identify what they wanted students to accomplish, they began to realize they didn't have a way to deal with those intangible states called attitudes and feelings. "How do I write effective objectives?" they would ask. "I want trainees to develop a favorable attitude toward work," they would tell me, or "I want students to develop an appreciation for music."

The concerns were reasonable, but presented a problem because the mindset from which they sprang was process-oriented. *Developing* an attitude is hardly the same as *having* that attitude. Confusing an outcome with the process for accomplishing it leads people to want to take action before knowing what that action is expected to accomplish. This cart-before-the-horse approach is like constructing a building before having any idea what the completed structure is to look like.

I once had the good fortune to consult with two Catholic priests eager to increase their congregations' reverence. These were dedicated men willing to do almost anything to accomplish their goal. "We'll put in guitar music, if that's what it takes," one quipped. "We'll even put in bucket seats if that will help," added the other. They were ready to *do* something. Without a clear picture of what "reverence" would look and feel like, though, "doing something" would have been premature.

Fortunately, I had been tinkering with an approach for dealing with abstractions such as "reverence." The procedure, which I called goal analysis, simply asked one to describe how successful accomplishment of a goal might be recognized. So we began a goal analysis of "be reverent." This involved describing how the priests would recognize reverence if they saw it. It wasn't easy, and they weren't entirely successful. But as they described manifestations of reverence, they learned they were farther along in their quest than they had imagined. Bucket seats weren't necessary.

This sort of experience wasn't rare; people were and are almost always eager to take action before painting a picture of their target. They put the cart before the horse—describing *means* for reaching as-yet undefined *ends*. What to do? In spare moments I began crafting a book on the subject. But I couldn't simply tell readers, "Look. It's easy. Just write an operational definition of the attitude you want to achieve." That might lead to a brisk one-paragraph book, but it wouldn't help people develop the skill. Besides, most had never heard of operational definitions. The solution was to lay out a step-by-step procedure that could be understood and practiced.

Though the issue had nagged at me since the appearance of the objectives book ten years earlier, *Goal Analysis* wasn't published until 1972. The world didn't allow me a "time out" to write merely because I felt I had something to say.

nineteen

Insights from the Vineyard

URING THE DECADES THAT FOLLOWED, the consulting calendar stayed pretty full, and I was now committed to toiling in the vineyards of training and the broader field of human performance. Fortunately, the projects ranged widely, leading to further expansion of my understanding of how the world worked or to confirmation of previous insights.

For example, in 1967 I was asked to serve as part-time Director of Research for the Aerospace Education Foundation (AEF), a subsidiary of the Air Force Association (AFA). What possible need could the AEF have for a research director—even part-time? The answer was simple. Both the AFA and the AEF were seriously interested in improving public education. Their perception was that the graduates of our high schools were becoming less and less able to function successfully in the world around them. As evidence, they cited the escalating resources devoted to teaching high school graduates basic life skills—like reading and writing.

As I said, I was thrust into this exhilarating environment as Director of Research. I didn't do any actual research though. Mainly, I reviewed and evaluated research relevant to AEF interests, and wrote briefs describing my reactions to research proposals.

One of the AEF's major projects involved the creation and presentation in 1968 of an exhibition called The National Laboratory for the Advancement of Education. The idea was to put examples of successful instructional practices on public display to serve as a model. Ten examples of exemplary instruction were selected from around the country, and transported—classrooms, teachers, students, and equipment—to the Washington exhibition hall. There for all to see were living examples of outstanding instructional practices—projects actually in operation.

It was a stunning event. Professionally produced by the AFA and attended by several hundred noted researchers, educators, and government representatives, ideas ricocheted around the rooms like laser beams in a sealed container. Nobody left untouched by the classroom demonstrations or the young students' enthusiasm. It was truly a celebration of academic excellence, and we all learned that bright spots do exist among the mediocre and dismal. Two great exhibits in particular illustrated the real-world possibilities of systematic instructional design.

Flying high

One project involved students judged to be largely "unteachable." The high school was located in a poor neighborhood in northern California, where two teachers of one class said to their students, in effect, "We're going to throw out this irrelevant school curriculum. Instead, we're going to teach you how to fly airplanes." That, by itself, attracted the students' attention and aroused their curiosity.

First, students were taken for a flight in one of the four-seat airplanes offered by local private aviation. After a few minutes in the air, each student took a turn at piloting the plane. They didn't know how to take off and land, of course, but it doesn't take much to learn to hold a small plane level in smooth air. Imagine the thrill. They were not only flying, they were in control. Result? When they returned to earth, they became instant heroes in their neighborhoods.

Now the plot thickened. To stay a hero, they had to stay in the curriculum. But a strange thing happened to that "boring" curriculum. To fly a plane, they had to learn to read a map. To fly a plane, they had to learn to speak clear English into the radio. They had to learn to compute distances and fuel loads. They had to learn to read. In other words, they had to learn many of the things taught in that old "irrelevant" curriculum—except that much of the old content now became a matter of life or death. Equally significant, they weren't just learning *about* these things—they were learning to *do* them.

Did this program work? The final report ("Learning Through Aviation," by Lee Conway, 1970), reported improvement in attendance, reading ability, general ability level, and grades (which improved in the students' other courses as well). There were *no dropouts* from the aviation program, in contrast with a 20 percent dropout rate from the control group. The school average absentee rate was 14 percent, but only 2 percent for the flight group. The report stated, "Academic as well as character growth has occurred among the majority of flight project students in the course of the year."

Several factors contributed to the success. The students' initial learning event was flying an airplane. Thus they experienced an airplane hands-on (the major objective of the learning) *before* facing the theory of flight, which, at that moment, had no relevance for them. They got to fly, talk about the thrill of flying, and talk to professional pilots. Next, they were given the freedom to learn what they felt they needed to master the assignments (map-reading, speaking, reading, measuring, etc.)

Moreover, they were encouraged to put their learning into practice on real-world problems. When I walked into the classroom one day not one student even looked up; they were too busy disassembling aircraft engines and reading blueprints. Boys and girls were on hands and knees with screwdrivers and wrenches in hand—completely engrossed.

But here's the big AHA! The same results could be achieved with subjects other than piloting an aircraft. Imagine being told, for example, "We're going to write and produce a motion picture, and you're all going to be in it." Students would have to learn to speak, read, write, and measure distances—that is, they'd have to develop the same skills needed for success in many of life's occupations—but now there would be an immediate purpose for learning them. Many other real-world professions might be used as the motivation for learning core skills—like restaurant management, television production, auto repair, or acting. The conclusion: want to get rid of a truancy "problem"? Give the curriculum a purpose relevant to the lives of the students.

What happened to this project? It was cancelled. My contacts confided that the project worked too well to be tolerated by other faculty and administrators. Unfortunately, the demise of the successful is not at all rare. I recall a high school teacher who accepted a class of "unteachable misfits" after others had declined. By the end of the school year she had succeeded so well her students' grades had improved, and truancy had all but disappeared. The students were so pleased they presented her with a substantial gift. How was she rewarded for her success by her administrators? She was pushed out of the school system. She'd made the mistake of proving them wrong.

Individualized instruction

Another "point of light" at the exhibition was imported from the frozen North. Thorwald Esbensen, Assistant Superintendent of Schools in Duluth, Minnesota, had decided to install an individualized curriculum for grades one through twelve. It was a bold move, especially for a small city with very old "egg-crate" schools. But "Tory" was a bold man and persevered. He began with grades five and six, and expanded to the grade on either side each year thereafter—first to grades 4 and 7, then 3 and 8, and so on.

Each school was divided into subject areas, with science rooms over here, the English room down the hall, etc. All students had a folder containing the "contracts" (objectives) they agreed to accomplish in each subject area. When ready to work on an English contract, they went to the English area, took their folder from the bin, and continued where they had left off. When they wanted to work on their science contract, they went to the science area and did the same. They were free to move about and decide how and when they would work toward accomplishment of their objectives. Teachers were always available to provide assistance or guidance.

Results were intriguing. Students were eager to get to school in the morning and reluctant to leave at the end of the day. Teachers actually complained about students not wanting to go home in the afternoons and about needing somebody to stay behind to keep an eye on them. The Fire Commissioner complained that students used the hallways as places to learn (imagine that!), as art students unrolled their butcher paper on the floor to paint murals and decorated the fire extinguishers with papier-mâché flowers.

There was another unexpected result. A subtle form of punishment had vanished. Typically, the consequence of completing one task was to be assigned a harder one (once again to be thrust from the known into the unknown). This was no longer true in the project schools. Instead, if it felt good to solve a certain class of problem, students could linger over those problems as long as they wanted. I talked with a young boy who had disassembled and reassembled a model steam engine several times—taking it apart, polishing the piston, then putting it back together again. He didn't have to do that. He lingered because it felt good, and because he wanted to savor his new skill. He was allowed to "love" the subjects he was learning about, rather than being forced to lock-step his way to the next subject after an arbitrary time period had passed. Watching the process was beauty in motion.

Sadly, as is so often the case, the project withered when its champion, Tory Esbensen, left the system. To make good ideas work after their originators have departed requires sustained effort and serious support from management. At the very least, good ideas must be written into policies confirming the idea to be "the way things are done."

It's not a secret

These were only two examples of the real-world applications of systematic instructional design. In the larger context, what excited many of us working in the field was seeing how the laws of learning could improve instructional effectiveness beyond our wildest dreams. Consider, for example, that in 1968, Lloyd Homme et al., published a paper describing their work with contingency management techniques (where rewards are made contingent on desired performance, rather than applied at random, or not at all), reporting that:

"With these kinds of procedures, it has been possible to keep preschool children responding eight hours a day and to teach phonic reading in a matter of days, rather than semesters or years."

In the same paper, the authors reported their ability to positively influence the development of "self-concept, love, and joy." And that was in 1968. To my knowledge, nobody else was concerned with the joy of learning!

Using more precise application of these same techniques at Stanford University, Dr. Albert Bandura reported being able to cure life-long phobias in a matter of hours.

There were, of course, critics who said, "I tried using those techniques, and they didn't work." These were undoubtedly examples of sloppy workmanship. These techniques work only if they are applied with a certain amount of precision. Put another way, the principles always work, but if incorrectly applied, they work to produce unwanted results.

Feeding a gift horse

A year earlier (1967), Air Force training personnel had noticed that, as a result of their own attempts to improve their instruction, they were delivering hundreds of well-crafted courses on as many subjects. They wondered whether some of these course materials might be of value to the public schools. "Why re-invent the wheel," went the thought, "when we have these fine materials we'd be happy to share?" The idea developed wings, and the Utah Project was born.

To test whether the materials would, in fact, be usable, five schools, ranging from a high school to a four-year college, volunteered to have three programs transferred to their institutions: Basic Electronics, Medical Laboratory Technician, and Aircraft Mechanics. This was the first organized transfer of course materials from Air Force to civilian classrooms.

A whirlwind of activity followed. Materials—books, manuals, slides, and teacher-training aids—were transferred to the schools in eight months. According to an AEF publication, this was ". . . unprecedented in an educational community which normally functions with lead times measured in years, if not decades." The materials were of high quality and welcomed by the school faculties. But even with the teacher aids provided, faculties were unsure of how to proceed. This was especially the case with materials intended for use in individualized settings. Instructional staffs had little or no experience with objective-based, individualized programs, and suitable instructor training did not exist.

Here was the challenge. After seeing the difficulty instructors were experiencing, the AEF asked if I would develop an instructor training program, and I agreed (1972). With Peter Pipe as co-author, we set out to fill the need. This was our opportunity to put into practice almost everything we thought we knew about making instruction effective, efficient, and elegant. We decided to create a workshop to model the instructional process we hoped others would emulate. It would teach by example, guaranteeing that students would experience the same performance-based environment they were being taught to re-create when they returned to their own classes. It would apply as many learning principles as possible and minimize obstacles between the learners and their learning.

Such an undertaking would require a radical departure from the traditional classroom. Rather than sitting at desks in rows facing the front, participants would sit at tables facing in various directions—more like a card party than a theater. There would be no "front" to the room. That alone would make it difficult for an instructor to lecture to the entire group, rather than coach individual trainees. It would also prevent the triggering of the "us-against-them" mindset found in the theatrical-style classroom.

We conducted a tryout of the entire workshop at one of the Utah vocational schools. This was no small courtesy, as we required facilities and services for three full weeks. We were confident participants would finish the modules in less time, but we weren't taking any chances.

Peter and I struggled with the issue of naming the workshop. Not wanting to be guilty of inventing unnecessary new jargon, we decided to use words already in the lexicon of the training world. We named the workshop *Criterion-Referenced Instruction*, or *CRI*. We were not satisfied with our final choice, but at least it suggested the essential characteristic of the product.

With materials and participants in place, the tryout began. After an initial orientation session, trainees were told they could study and practice until ready to demonstrate competence of a module's objective. When their performance met or exceeded the objective's criteria, they would be encouraged to advance to the next module. We then removed ourselves from the path of learning and let them begin work on their first module.

That was the hard part—for us. Until that moment, we were in control. When the orientation session ended, however, we had to shut up and allow the focus of attention to shift to the students. Letting go was like going into free-fall. It was nail-biting time. Would students take control of their learning? Would they dare give up the habits learned in a lifetime of theatrical classrooms, where learning events and their duration were orchestrated for them?

There was some initial hesitation as participants glanced left and right to see what others would do. They were thinking (we learned through de-briefings), "Are these guys really *serious* about our taking control of our own learning?" Each participant seemed to be waiting for someone else to make the first move. They looked at us to take charge, but we looked the other way. It was their turn. Though prior experience convinced me there would be no motivation problems, we were still somewhat apprehensive. We needn't have been.

Before long, they decided we were indeed serious about the "rules," and dug in. From then on, there was no stopping them. Nor did we have to wonder about our own usefulness in the classroom. There was plenty for us to do. Answer questions, provide materials, review accomplishments, explain a concept, offer additional examples, and just talk with someone about applying the concepts to his/her own work environment.

Peter and I learned as much as the participants did. We learned, for example, that there was no need to keep track of individual module-completion times. It didn't matter if one participant required more, or less, time than another to reach competence. Our Master Progress Plotter showed at a glance how each was progressing and whether anyone needed assistance. We learned how to let go and allow the course procedures to work their magic. We learned to trust the participants to work and take breaks when they felt the need. They worked hard, not to please us, but to achieve the rewards experienced when checking off another completed module and applying another new skill.

When it was over and the minor bugs were vanquished, we delivered the revised materials to the AEF for their use. To our knowledge, this was the first criterion-referenced, self-paced approach directed at teaching instructors to conduct criterion-referenced, self-paced courses. It was a major milestone.

twenty

Taking the Plunge

ENCOURAGED BY AEF PRINCIPALS JIM STRAUBEL AND MIKE NISOS, I decided to modify the CRI workshop materials and make them available to the corporate and military arenas. The decision was not easy, as it would require a significant investment by our tiny corporation. Even so, I decided to take the risk. Peter Pipe agreed to continue as co-author. This was an opportunity for Peter and me to apply everything we'd learned so far, and I wasn't inclined to turn a deaf ear when that opportunity knocked.

Suddenly I was not only an entrepreneur, but a publisher and distributor as well. More hands and hours were needed; there was much to learn and do to prepare the materials for public use. It was a busy time.

The first public CRI workshop was offered in the summer of 1974. Just locating a hotel willing to tie up a block of sleeping and meeting rooms for three weeks was a challenge. The Villa Hotel in San Mateo, California was willing to give it a try, however, so we were off. (To offer perspective, room rates were $16 per night for a single; $21 for a double. The enrollment fee was $850 for the entire three-week workshop.)

I engaged three course managers to work with up to twenty-four participants. After spreading the word about the coming workshop through a one-page flyer, another nail-biting wait followed. Happily, enrollments came in, and Margo Murray (then Margo Hicks), David Cram, and I moved into the hotel along with the participants, where we pioneered the first public Criterion-Referenced Instruction Workshop. (We always stayed at the workshop hotel, whether or not it was within driving distance of home.)

The workshop went fine . . . until the last day. Our initial brochure said, ". . . some participants will finish in 15 days while others will romp through in 10 or 11 . . ." That's exactly what happened. At our foolishly scheduled end-of-course luncheon, there was hardly anybody left. By then, most had completed the workshop and gone home, just as we'd planned.

A few observations. It took participants about a day and a half to develop the new habit of taking charge of their own learning—to *believe* what we had explained at the orientation session (we now know how to make that happen in just a few minutes). But from then on, they had no problem deciding what activity would best move them toward accomplishment of an objective. Sometimes they worked on their own, sometimes with another participant or course manager. Sometimes a group discussion sprouted.

The workshop was characterized by constant activity. Study a module, practice the skill, go to the bin for a Skill Check (performance test) or resource, go to the coffee room for coffee or soda, watch one of the videos, practice a skill with another participant, consult with a course manager, take a break. The low buzz of conversation was occasionally punctuated by a few seconds of spontaneous laughter.

We had announced at the beginning of the workshop that course managers would be on the premises from 8:30 a.m. until 4:30 p.m., and that participants were free to come and go as they pleased. For several days, everyone arrived by 8:30. Those arriving a bit later apologized for being late. We learned to explain that in a self-paced, performance-based course, there is no "late." That was a relief to those who felt themselves to be "afternoon learners."

"Late," we explained, is a condition legislated into, or out of, existence by the course rules—like truancy. The "work when you're ready" rule can't always be adopted, of course, especially if an activity (e.g., time in a simulator) requires advance scheduling. When it *can* be applied, however, it removes yet another obstacle to learning.

There was a minor problem—some participants forgot to take breaks. They became so engrossed in their self-directed activity they often forgot to pace themselves. Much to our surprise, we found ourselves having to butt in on participants we judged to be working too hard for too long. What a concept!

Soon participants began requesting that we leave the workshop rooms unlocked at the end of the afternoon—many wanted to work beyond 4:30 p.m. To encourage them to leave, course managers would leave at 4:30 so no one would be available to provide assistance or module signoffs. It made no difference—many participants stayed anyhow.

I tried to sensitize course managers to identify and eliminate as many obstacles as possible. A few rules: If someone hands you a breath mint, use it—no questions asked. Another rule had to do with hovering behavior—leaning over the shoulder of a participant while talking. The rule: If you see another course manager hovering (i.e., assuming the "vulture" position), either call it to his or her attention or slide a chair under his/her butt. That rule kept us on an equal level with the students and helped avoid an us-against-them atmosphere.

These may seem like trivial practices, but they modeled the sentiment we wanted to convey: that each of us was a resource from whom others could learn.

Decision time

Before long, requests for in-house workshops taxed our resources, forcing me to make a decision about how to add course managers. Engage them as self-employed professionals, or put them on the payroll as full-time employees? I couldn't see allowing my life forces to drain into the ground doing management chores, so I opted to engage additional self-employed professionals.

That turned out to be the right decision. Except when conducting workshops, they could work from their home offices rather than in a central cubicle farm. Between workshops, they could apply their skills to projects in the real world, thereby gaining more relevant experience to apply at the next workshop. They wouldn't get stale—a strong plus. The downside was that intra-day face-to-face contact and information exchange wasn't possible among Associates scattered around the world. Such exchanges occurred during workshops, but only during stolen moments.

Bootstrapping

Somehow, we had to be able to review and grow our skills on a more regular basis. As a partial solution, I initiated a more-or-less annual four-day Update Seminar during which we could share information and learn and practice new and old skills. To entice Associates to attend (I certainly wasn't going to book a hotel in Cleveland!), I booked sessions at a secluded resort in Hawaii—no TV, no telephones.

For me, these seminars were the highlight of the year. We honed our skills, presented information about new developments, shared information about experiences with clients, and continued bonding during relaxing evenings. It was a good investment—better than investing in ego-salving, but unnecessary, office trappings.

One year, I coaxed Dr. Albert Bandura into sharing his wisdom with our group. Doing so, however, required that we travel to his natural habitat in Palo Alto. We were more than willing to make the "sacrifice," and gladly basked in the opportunity to sit at his feet while he described his work and answered our questions.

Faulty perceptions

One may wonder why, if it works so well, the performance-based, self-paced approach hasn't been more widely adopted? There are several reasons. Prominent among them is that many instructors are reluctant to give up their "platform." In the instructor-dominated classroom they are the kings and queens of all they survey. They decide what is to be taught, how long they will dwell on each topic, which war stories they will tell, and what grades they will assign. That's a lot to give up. I was reluctant to give it up too, until I actually experienced the joys of the performance-based, self-paced approach. I still enjoy making presentations on occasion, but I'd never be comfortable returning to the theatrical mode of teaching.

One of the obstacles hindering others from adopting a self-directed, performance-based system relates to class control. Our participants move about at will and see others doing the same. The occasional visitor often sees a lack of control—a seeming lack of "discipline"—in our classrooms. "How do you get students to work?" they ask. "How do you keep order and control?" This is hardly a surprising question coming from people with lifetimes of experiences in the instructor-dominated classroom. When those questions are asked by participants, we ask participants to reflect on their own experience during the workshop. We ask them why they don't simply sit and goof off—why they choose to work so hard that we have to remind them to take breaks.

"But how do you keep control of the process?" some persist. In response, we point to their own Personal Progress Guides, the chart showing course manager initials besides completed modules. It's rewarding to garner those initials—it means they've demonstrated their accomplishment of another objective. This is why we can stand aside to let the process happen; it's why we can comfortably ignore instances of what looks like coasting behavior.

When Hawaii installed a program similar to ours in some of their schools, a few of the military parents became livid over the idea of giving students partial control of their own learning. "There's no discipline!" they complained when seeing students working under the tables or out in the courtyard. To them, discipline apparently equated to students sitting in rows facing the front of the room. Though there was total control of the process in the project schools at all times, these parents saw only chaos. They completely failed to see the "command and control" structure—which was *intended* to be invisible.

A strategic decision

During the years that followed, we refined the CRI materials and procedures, published improved editions, and reduced the length of the workshop from three weeks to two. Most participants still complete their work in less than the time allotted, partly because they've learned from colleagues preceding them, or read the resource books, or because the streamlined procedures have greased their way.

While developing CRI, we had decided to omit modules directed specifically at module development (writing), because only a small percentage of those who deliver instruction actually develop it. Those people deserved special attention, so in 1977 I created the two-week *Instructional Module Development Workshop (IMD)*.

As the IMD workshop progresses, participants develop and try out at least two work-related modules on fellow participants. It is always interesting to watch them develop a module for instruction that currently requires two to six hours to teach in a standard classroom. The look of disappointment on some of their faces as they realize their new module will require only a few minutes to learn is priceless. (Later, they learn to rejoice in it.) This realization was and is often accompanied by wringing of hands and the lament, "What will my supervisor say when he/she finds out his/her one-day course can be learned in less than an hour?" It is a powerful confirmation of the amount of unnecessary fluff contained in much of what passes for instruction.

How do you write a book?

During the years spanning publication of one or more books and workshops, I continued to tell myself I wasn't a real writer—that *real* writers sit down at their keyboards and instantly begin banging out words and sentences. I struggled—still do. "Writer" wasn't part of my self-image. I wrote because I had to, not because I thought I knew how. That, of course, was another unexamined assumption—I was confusing task difficulty with skill level. Thanks to Bandura's work on self-efficacy, I now know better. Skill level shouldn't be judged by performance difficulty. Lots of things are hard to learn or hard to do. Get over it . . . and get on with it! Writing may be hard work, but that shouldn't mean you can't learn to do it well, or that you aren't already doing it well.

After several of my books were successfully published, however, people kept asking, "How do you *do* that?" or, "I've got an idea for a book I want to write. How do I start?" Why are they asking *me*? I wondered. Ask a *real* writer. The question was asked so often I developed a two-question response to get the curious started on their writing projects.

"Who will your book be for?" I'd ask. That took most inquirers aback. They hadn't thought about that. They wanted to write a book and reveal everything they knew about a topic. Period.

Next question. What do you want the book to accomplish? "Accomplish? I want to write a book." End of story.

Prodding, I'd ask, "Do you want it to inform, or entertain, or mystify, or motivate, or instruct? What?" Usually that was enough to send them away to think more constructively about their project.

But I also kept tossing notes about book-writing into a folder. At long last, I opened the folder and started drafting a book on how to write a book. *The How To Write a Book Book* was not about what to write, or about how to write fiction (I knew nothing about that topic until years later): it was about how to get started, keep going, conduct manuscript tryouts, and recognize when the book was finished. (Which reminds me of an old joke: Question: When is your book finished? Answer: When an editor tears it out of your hands.)

An odd thing happened when I set out to publish the book. By some long-forgotten means, I found myself with a contract in hand from a major publisher. Just as I was about to sign it, I noticed a clause telling me the publisher reserved the right to modify the content. Oh-oh. I called to verify my understanding. Sure enough, the publisher wanted to change the chapter on how to get a non-fiction manuscript published—to change it from the writer's point of view to the publisher's point of view. Oh? That would, of course, have defeated the purpose of the book, so I tore up the contract and published it myself in 1986. (It is now published by CEP Press.)

It was a gratifying project; a number of people have told me the book stimulated them to get started on their own, and the mail has delivered several published books resulting from their efforts.

(By the way, if you've ever wondered about the distinction between writers and authors: A writer writes; an author is a published writer.)

A glitch in time

Life lurched along relatively smoothly until 1980, when my thirty-two-year-old marriage frayed around the edges. It had kind of worn itself out, and reluctantly we decided to part. What followed was maximum gloom, during which little work was accomplished. Lifting a pencil became a major undertaking; productive thought became impossible.

That dismal state persisted until an angel appeared in the form of a saleswoman in a furniture-store I chanced to enter when foraging for replacement furniture. She immediately diagnosed my plight, took me under her wing, and told me how to begin climbing the ladder back to the surface of life. She told me about books to read—and avoid—about how to proceed, and about how long the healing would take. I wish I'd taken her name; I'd like to tell her how she changed my life.

Then, at the annual NSPI Conference a few months later, the unexpected happened. I had occasion to coordinate NSPI committee chores with a woman I had spoken to at previous Conferences— she was VP in charge of the upcoming Conference, and I was the Awards Chair. During those periodic meetings, a spark ignited. One thing led to another and eventually we raised the (scary) issue of marriage. That wasn't easy for me. Eileen was considerably younger than I— still is—and I was afraid if I married her I might be arrested for contributing to the delinquency of a minor. (It took me almost four years to get over it.) Twenty-two years of happy marriage later, I still refer to her as my "teenager." (One of the projects on our back burner is a book on age-disparate marriages. There are more of those around than you might think.)

Move is still a four-letter word

Shortly after being married to the strains of a ukulele (barefoot on the beach of Kona—at sunset), we left Silicon Valley and moved to the desert of Arizona (1982). After sampling the area, we decided to settle in Carefree, what was then a sleepy little community north of Phoenix. How sleepy? "Downtown" is the intersection of Ho and Hum Streets (honest!), our downtown office is on Easy Street, and the banks are on Wampum Way. Even so, the laid-back street names didn't work. We work harder and longer hours than before the move.

Convinced we had arrived at "Here," we began digging in. Armed with blueprints for the extensive renovations we planned, we trotted across the street to show our neighbors how we would transform our brand new tract house into one consistent with other houses on the street. They weren't too anxious to open their door—they thought we'd arrived with an armload of religious pamphlets. Once we introduced ourselves, all was well and they braced themselves for the forthcoming construction.

Though we're located in the middle of nowhere—third cactus on the left—there are distinct advantages. The existence of fax, e-mail, internet, and telephone have practically eliminated the need for uncomfortable air travel, and the commute from home to office is only about forty-seven seconds. Plus, we no longer need a snow shovel

or lawn mower. Most importantly, we've moved away from Ground
Zero West.

twenty-one

We're All Alike

D
URING THE YEARS FOLLOWING THE INTRODUCTION of the CRI
Workshop, we took it and the other workshops to other
countries. We were apprehensive at first, having often been
told that it wouldn't work in this or that country because of significant
cultural differences. "People are different," we were told. "Their
cultures are too different to accept a self-paced format." We went
anyhow.

Not long after the first public CRI workshops, I contracted to
conduct the CRI workshop in Mexico City for a group of corporate
clients. Associate Paul Whitmore and I packed our bags and headed
South of the Border. This would be the first "foreign" test of the
workshop and we wondered how well it would fit into the Mexican
culture. We didn't have to wonder long.

The workshop was to be conducted in a hacienda surrounding
a tree-dotted courtyard. It was a pleasant environment. Very
Mexican, very comfortable. Before the workshop began, our

Mexican host took me aside.

"You realize, Doctor Mager, that the Mexican culture is different from your own." I had no idea where he was headed, so I just waited. "Yes," he continued. "Our culture is more formal than yours—our students demand lectures."

I thought about that while formulating a response. "I understand," I finally said. "Suppose we conduct the workshop according to its usual procedures, except that each afternoon from three to four p.m. I will offer a lecture."

That satisfied our host and he agreed to the proposal. The first afternoon at three I lectured on one of the workshop topics. When I finished, everyone gathered around to tell me how wonderful it was. The next afternoon only half the class showed up. Only partially daunted, I lectured again. When I finished, everyone again gathered around to tell me how wonderful it was.

The next afternoon, no one showed up and our host trolled the courtyard for attendees. By then, participants were convinced they didn't need to work inside a classroom or listen to a lecture when they could work under a tree in the courtyard. Our host discovered that, given the opportunity to direct their own learning, the people of his culture were the same as anyone else. We saw once again that the laws of nature are universal. At that point the lecture series was cancelled.

("Except in Hawaii," wrote a reviewer of an earlier draft of this book. "Getting Hawaiian course developers to do anything was one of my biggest challenges. They simply wanted to eat, sing, laugh, and fish. By the end of the workshop, they had *me* doing thosethings. It wasn't clear whose behavior was changed for the better.")

The workshops have since been conducted in Europe, Scandinavia, South America, South Africa, the Middle East, and Asia. The results are always the same: With the exception of minor adjustments for local customs, participants are eager to take hold of their own learning, and work as long as they are allowed to do so.

When visiting an on-going workshop in Paris, for example, we discovered that the daily lunch was catered by the workshop host. (Our normal practice is to encourage participants to lunch where and when they please.) We were told it was "just a *small* lunch," and were invited to partake. We quickly learned this was to be the French version of a "small lunch"—several courses, including wines and dessert. Oof!

Mike Bebb, our then-South African representative and course manager, reported this experience with CRI in Nepal. At the time, there was a two-year qualifying course for paper mill technicians operating in England. To qualify, candidates were required to pass a "City and Guilds" exam. But two years seemed a long time, considering the content to be mastered by the workers in Nepal. Convinced he could do better, Mike created a criterion-referenced, self-paced course to qualify technicians for a specific Nepalese paper mill.

When the first group completed the course, Mike reported the trainees required an average of only *six weeks* to qualify—not two years. This result is a little misleading since Mike was training operators for a specific mill and the training offered in the UK was broader in scope. Nonetheless, the result was surprising and caused considerable consternation in political circles. The workers weren't expected to be able to learn much of anything at that time because they weren't white—for them to become successful in such a short time was a bit unsettling to the establishment. (One thing led to another, and some time later Mike and his wife emigrated to New Zealand.)

The CRI approach, we felt, would face its most stringent cultural challenge when Eileen and I headed to Beijing in 1996 to conduct the "Training Manager Workshop." Our trainees included training managers from China, as well as Singapore and Hong Kong. Four were from India, and one came from the United States (the only "foreign" trainee in the group). Course procedures for this five-day, self-paced, criterion-referenced workshop are similar to those of the CRI workshop, so we were a bit apprehensive about how the workshop structure would be accepted. Again, we needn't have worried.

Participants offered no resistance to the course procedures. They took control of their learning and progressed as rapidly as any American group. Typically, when English is their second language, participants are hesitant to speak it until they begin to trust the environment. That happened in the Beijing workshop, too, even with four simultaneous interpreters standing by. By the third day, most were willing to try speaking to us without the help of an interpreter.

On the fourth day, something incredible happened. The oldest participant had traveled from the north of China with three of his younger colleagues. Late on Thursday morning they all disappeared. An hour later, they returned carrying nine large watermelons and presented these as a token of their respect and appreciation. Wow!

The number nine is significant, we learned. Nine is the largest single-digit number and carries special meaning in China. When visiting the Forbidden City, for example, one finds nine rows of nine bolts each on the Emperor's doors. Eight is a rather special number as well, but not as special as nine. We felt honored, and tried to show our own appreciation by eating as much watermelon as our stomachs would tolerate. Oof again!

When we asked participants their reactions to the workshop format we were told it was consistent with Buddhist philosophy. No wonder they had no difficulty taking hold!

At the end of the workshop, we hosted dinner and carousing at a German restaurant. The highlight of the evening occurred when Eileen stood, and, without musical accompaniment, sang some of the participants' favorite songs—in Mandarin! Jaws dropped in surprise—and pleasure—over someone taking the trouble to learn something of their language.

These workshops continue to be conducted in a wide variety of countries, and always re-confirm that the laws of nature are universal. People wear different clothing, speak different languages, and observe different customs, but they're all alike in that they all behave according to the laws of nature. People everywhere try to avoid situations they find punishing, and try to spend as much time as possible in circumstances they find satisfying.

When pondering the consequences of a shrinking planet, that's a wonderful thing to know.

twenty-two

Light Heart and Lead Feet

FLASHBACK. NINETEEN SEVENTY-EIGHT FOUND ME leading a sedentary life at the typewriter and in serious need of exercise. I was fifty-five years old and getting creaky. But finding an exercise I would stick to was not easy. Avoiding exercise was. You know how it is . . . I can't play tennis today because my partner died. Golf? It's too windy. How about going to the gym? Sorry, it's raining way too hard. Jogging? Aw, it's too hot.

To attack the problem I listed the characteristics of an exercise interesting enough to induce me to persevere. The main items: (a) an exercise that would occupy the mind, (b) that could be done at home, (c) that wouldn't need a partner or team, and (d) would not require expensive equipment.

What could possibly fill those requirements? I tried, but couldn't think of a thing. Six weeks later it came to me—tap dancing. That would meet all the requirements. But that was the easy part. To continue the quest I needed a dancing instructor. Where are they hidden? The Yellow Pages of the phone book, of course. That began an intimidating foray. Some of the ads displayed line drawings of little girls in tutus, but I couldn't help imagining myself standing in the middle of that line of urchins—with or without tutu. It took another six weeks to gather the nerve to pick up the phone.

A female voice answered. I asked her if they taught tap.

"Yes, we do."

"To old people?"

"How old are you talking about?"

"I'm fifty-five," I replied.

"That's nothing," she said, her voice smiling. "Your instructor is sixty-five . . . and our oldest student is eighty-five." I wondered whether she could feel me relaxing.

I signed up and began weekly private lessons. It was everything I hoped for—I could practice at home, alone, at my convenience, and needed only a tape player and a pair of shoes. But it was slow going. I felt like an elephant. It wasn't until six months later I suddenly found myself on my toes, after which I became a terror on the dance floor. I'd break into tap on any hard surface I chanced to be standing on, even hotel bathrooms and hard-surfaced elevators.

That worked well until we moved to Arizona. I enrolled for a tap class consisting of two dozen women (most over 65 with terrific legs), and me. They're great people, but somewhat less interested in dancing than schmoozing. As I was there for the exercise, I switched to a private lesson at the same studio.

Though my goal was exercise, the regular practice led to development of a reasonable amount of skill. Why not put it to use?

It happened that for five consecutive years (1990–95), my wife and I performed in an annual variety show at Phoenix Symphony Hall. My wife sang (she's a super soprano), and I did a ventriloquist act. One year I challenged myself with a difficult goal. I would create an act during which I would carry a puppet and ventriloquize while tap dancing around the stage. It seemed impossible, but what the heck. It was a sizable challenge and worth a try.

After lots and lots of practice, the act began working and we were off to Symphony Hall. As the act was well received, I decided to try it during the passenger talent show on our next cruise. Fortunately, the sea was relatively calm and I didn't fall down. The audience seemed to enjoy the idiot tap dancing around the stage while arguing with a puppet. (The practice video shows I needed another month of practice to make it look relaxed and spontaneous.) The challenge, however, was exhilarating and served its purpose. Who says exercise has to be boring? I continued to dance with the shapely-legged women, and joined them occasionally for dance gigs at local venues. It was great fun and an aid to healthy living.

This dancing episode may seem irrelevant to the story, but it provided value far beyond simple exercise. One of the prevailing messages perpetuated by the media and other elements in our society is that old people should know their place. Sex? Why, they should be ashamed of themselves for even thinking about it! Instead, they should go away and die on an ice floe somewhere. They shouldn't be taking up valuable space and squandering their children's inheritances. And they certainly shouldn't be tap dancing their way around the world. When I talk of my own plans for the future, the raised eyebrows of the younger generation seem to be saying, "What? *You're* making plans for the future—at *your* age?" But why not? When George Burns contracted to perform at the London Palladium during his 100th year, the event was greeted more often with laughter than admiration. Why is that?

At what age are *you* planning to stop having fun?

So dancing with those women was nothing short of inspiring. Rather than sit around doing grandma things, they leaped and whirled about in tap shoes, laughing and making plans for public performances. The group I danced with has so far traveled to Russia, Spain, and Australia, and are planning more. Their performances in Moscow brought Russian women to tears as they watched these shapely American women exercising a skill—and freedom—they could only dream about.

There was another unexpected lesson from the episode. The eighty-five-year-old dancer in California I mentioned earlier modeled yet another inspiring accomplishment. When she began dance lessons, she often fell down while trying to execute a turn. Six months later she no longer fell down! Her balance had improved as she practiced. The message? Apparently we have more control over our health and physical capabilities than we are led to believe. (Of *course* the condition of our inner ears influences our balance—but it's not the *only* influence.) Expectations can influence performance, and unexamined beliefs can shackle performance as surely as handcuffs.

twenty-three

A Novel Idea

JUMP AHEAD TO THE YEAR 1998. I was exhausted from a busy career and what seemed a lifetime of traveling in airplane seats designed by crazed thimble manufacturers. I had gone glassy-eyed from writing new editions of all the books in the Mager Six-Pack—again. (Writing is still hard work.) I'd been rooting about in the performance pastures for almost fifty years and found it harder and harder to poise my fingers over the keyboard. They began to rebel, and I was getting tired of their continual griping.

"Oh God, are we going to have to write *another* one?" one finger would ask its neighbor.

"Looks like it," the other would reply. "Why don't we just go limp and see what he does about *that*!"

Boredom set in. My wife suggested possible hobbies—model airplanes, elephant skinning, gun running, alligator wrestling—but nothing caught my interest.

One day, during lunch with my wife and a local friend, something incredible happened. As the two women talked, the pinball flipper whacked an idea for a story right into my head. I had no idea where it came from, or why; to that moment, I'd never had aspirations as a novelist. But the idea seemed too good to abandon. Just thinking about some of the scenes made me laugh. The rest, as they say, is history.

Though I approached this new craft as a rabbit might approach a porcupine, I was soon hooked and became completely absorbed in writing the story. It filled me with energy. I wrote mornings, afternoons, and sometimes evenings. My wife was ecstatic; I'd found something absorbing to do and had come back to life. The smile count—both hers and mine—went way up.

I didn't know anything about the rules of the novelist's craft, but I didn't let that stop me. I kept writing almost as fast as my fingers would move. They stopped complaining about the hard work, and when pressed into writing love scenes, they communicated their enthusiasm by typing "More! More!" down the page. (Perhaps that comment will be easier understood if I tell you that the book is called *The Steamy Novel*. It's about a technical writer who decides to write a steamy novel to counter his boredom, and whose first two badly-written pages become a portal through which he enters a new life and finds romance along the way.)

While writing the first draft of that first novel, I joined a local writers' group populated by writers who *write*. Constantly. Several have published more than three or four dozen novels, and all are willing to share their wisdom (so long as the sharing doesn't impinge on their writing time). Little by little, I began learning the craft.

I finished a draft of the first novel and, after re-writing it a time or three, plunged into a second book I was sure would be a romance novel. Instead, it turned out to be a "contemporary woman-in-jeopardy love story," but not a "romance" (the world of fiction has more categories and rules than a centipede has toes). That was followed by a full-length serial killer crime story, which required significant research that was just as interesting as the writing. (As a result, I know more about crematories than the average bear. For example, did you know that—never mind.)

When I wrote the first draft of this book, I wrote, "None of those manuscripts have as yet been published . . ." Ha! I'm pleased to report that's no longer true. A month later I signed a contract, as a result of which my crime novel, *Killer In Our Midst*, is now published. Currently, I'm re-writing the other two books and collecting characters for another. Some day, you may have an opportunity to chuckle and pant your way through *The Steamy Novel*, too.

Finally, though I can't explain why it took so long, I've at last realized that "Here" is a moving target.

Now it's your turn. Go *do something*.

"here" is still a
moving target

LOOKING OVER A SHOULDER, I notice my journey from there to here has had its share of twists and turns—as most life journeys do. That's a wonderful thing. Not everyone is fortunate enough to live in a country offering the freedom to pursue their dreams as they respond to the bumps and pings of their lives— to live in an environment where "Here" is allowed to be a moving target.

If you've survived the tumultuous years of the teens, you realize that the amount of freedom you enjoy is—in part—self-determined. For those who own but one pair of socks, the freedom to pick and choose among colors and patterns is severely limited. Similarly, for those owning only one skill, the freedom to choose among life's pathways is also limited. It's *skill* that gives us social mobility, not the color of our skin, the accent with which we speak, or the size of our bank account. It's *skill* that expands our freedom to strive for economic success, not "diversity," or political correctness, or any of the current or future buzzwords. *Skills* are what make self-reliance possible, and *skills* are what allow us to choose paths leading to success and contentment.

Living the lives of both serial occupationalist and serial hobbyist has led me to a varied and satisfying life, bumps and all. The journey itself has been—and still is—influenced by a variety of wonderful accomplices (some aware of their contributions, and others not). Some have been named in these pages. To name them all would be an impossible task because there are so many of them, and because some nudges were provided by that famous person—Anonymous. Many of them know who they are, and now will know their input and influence have been noticed and deeply appreciated.

It's time to end this chronicle—for now. But how? When the editors read an earlier draft, they whined, "But where's the exciting climax? The big finish? The surprise ending?"

Zheesh!

"Wait a minute," I retorted. "This isn't some sort of mystery where the identity of the miscreant is kept hidden until the last page. It isn't a romance novel where he and she predictably come together during the final pages. If it's any kind of love story, it's a love story with life, with learning, and with the joy of sharing insights with others."

It was a good try, but I'm not sure they're convinced even now. They'll just have to stay tuned as I continue thrashing about in the sandbox of life. I have new skills to learn, good deeds to perform— perhaps I'll slay a dragon and save a damsel in distress—or maybe write another page or two. But during the time remaining I intend to do *something*! In fact, I've been ordered not even to *think* about leaving the planet before the cows come home.

My dear wife threatens that if I die too soon, she'll kill me.

R. F. Mager
Carefree, Arizona

please note . . .

I T IS OFTEN SAID THAT GOOD WORKS DON'T GO UNPUNISHED . . . mine certainly don't! Any number of wastrels picked and pawed over these words. Some even snorted as they poked their pencils at deficient pages and misleading non-sequiturs. Their hearts were in the right place, though, so I suppose I should be grateful.

Matter of fact, the assistance of these people was enormously valuable. Indispensable. Many were even *there* when some of the described events occurred (I don't dare tell you how old that makes some of them), putting them in a position to correct facts and impressions accidentally slinking awry. Which they did, bless their souls, with great care. My appreciation is boundless.

Here they are, for all the world to see. David Cram, Joe Harless, Hilton Goldman, Eileen Mager, Dan Raymond, Peter Pipe, Seth Leibler, Ann Parkman, A. Robert Taylor, Randy Mager, and Libby Muelhaupt.

And what can I say about the editors—Suzanne Lawlor, Jill Russell, Mark Steudel—who slashed at my words, pounced on my paragraphs, and tsk-tsked at my grammatical indiscretions? Not enough. And, of course, a fanfare and deep bow to the folks at CEP Press for their courage in publishing this work.

Finally, I suppose I should mention it's customary for the author to take responsibility for remaining errors or lack of clarity. Well, all right . . .

R. F. Mager
March, 2003

postscript to the author

DEAR BOB:

Your publisher sent a draft of your latest offering, *Life in the Pinball Machine*. I suspect they want a favorable blurb for the book jacket, something like: Valuable life lessons from a master or If you don't buy this book you'll be sorry or Sliced bread is nothing compared to this book.

I might do that. But first, I feel compelled to send you my private reaction. First off, why didn't you tell me these life lessons and astute observations when I needed them? (Maybe you did and I wasn't listening.)

For example, why didn't you tell me always to be alert to a possible hidden agenda because there usually is one? I learned this too late to avoid years spent working merrily along on projects only to find snakes lurking in the weeds. Boy, could I ever tell you war stories about that.

I could have really benefited from realizing what you so clearly point out: we don't have to do a whole heckuva lot to motivate students. If the content of instruction is relevant, we engineer success with effective instruction and get the students doing something as soon as possible. I also now know that, but am sorry to say most educators and trainers still don't.

I suppose I now know we can't help what life presents, but we can control how we respond. And when in doubt, DO something—carpe diem and all that. Your book brings these insights to life. You could have saved me lots of paralyzing inertia and useless raging against the wind if you'd been thoughtful enough to tell me to lower my voice and get on with it.

Over the years, I've watched you wow audiences with wit and wisdom. I read your elegantly penned books. I assumed you were merely a gifted speaker and writer. I didn't know until I read this book that these "gifts" were the result of painful analysis, design, tryout, and revision. I suppose it's like the old joke: How do you get to Carnegie Hall? Practice, man, practice. If you had told me that sooner, I might have worked harder and saved all that time spent being envious.

I loved what you said about skills—that they give us social mobility, expand our freedom, and lead to contentment. I wish I had said that first. (Perhaps I'll claim that I did.)

I've always figured we all had to decide early what we wanted to be when we grew up. It was interesting to see you haven't decided and don't plan to. Perhaps we've taken this single-minded goal-dedication thing too far when it comes to our own lives. It occurred to me that if Mager can learn to be a tap-dancing novel-writing ventriloquist (and who knows what next), maybe I can lose a pound or two and become a jockey.

Your publishers have my permission to say I called the book "valuable life lessons from a master" and that folks will be sorry if they don't buy it. But, old friend, I'm still weighing the comparative merits of the book and sliced bread. Tell them to hold off on that quote until I read the book again.

As ever,
Joe Harless

the "library"

Other Books by Robert F. Mager

Analyzing Performance Problems or You really oughta wanna, by Robert F. Mager and Peter Pipe, 1997, 1984, 1970.

How to Turn Learners On . . . without turning them off, 1997. Originally published as *Developing Attitude Toward Learning or Smats 'n' Smuts,* 1984, 1968.

Goal Analysis, 1997, 1984, 1972.

The How to Write a Book Book, 1991, 1986.

Killer in Our Midst, 2003.

Making Instruction Work, 1997, 1988.

Measuring Instructional Results or Got A Match? 1997, 1984. Originally published as *Measuring Instructional Intent,* 1973.

Preparing Instructional Objectives, 1997, 1984, 1975. Originally published as *Preparing Objectives for Programmed Instruction,* 1962.

Troubleshooting the Troubleshooting Course or Debug d'Bugs, 1982.

What Every Manager Should Know About Training or "I've Got a Training Problem," and Other Odd Ideas, 1999, 1992.

Index

CEP Workshops

CEP offers *the* industry-standard Mager Workshops for training and performance improvement professionals. Our workshops don't just tell you about CRI-based instruction; we teach you how to *apply* the methodology to training projects.

Criterion-Referenced Instruction by Robert F. Mager and Peter Pipe
The CRI Methodology Part 1: Analysis, Design and Evaluation

The Criterion-Referenced Instruction workshop will give you immediately applicable, practical skills in analysis, design and evaluation necessary to succeed in a state-of-the-art training and performance improvement department. You'll learn how to:

- Conduct in-depth analysis (including goal, performance and task analyses)
- Edit and derive clear and measurable objectives
- Draft effective procedural guides, skill checks, course scenarios and course maps
- Plan course evaluations
- Quickly evaluate existing materials and plan course improvements

Instructional Module Development by Robert F. Mager
The CRI Methodology Part 2: Development

In the follow-up workshop to CRI, you build on your CRI skills to:

- Draft, try out and revise at least two modules of instruction for a course you are developing
- Test modules with other participants
- Experience firsthand the tryout process from the student' point of view
- Learn by seeing instruction in a variety of formats and subject areas

The Training Manager Workshop by Robert F. Mager

Learn how to support the achievement of your organization's strategic goals by providing employees with the skills and motivation to perform their jobs to management's expectations. During the workshop, you will work on the following modules:

- Evaluate instructors' performance
- Evaluate proposals for services
- Plan course evaluations
- Review training development progress
- Assess media choices
- Review training modules
- Solve performance problems
- Identify job tasks
- Create effective objectives
- Identify prerequisite skills

For more information and a schedule of public workshops, visit www.cepworldwide.com or call us at 1-800-558-4CEP